Silencing the Serpent

How Christians Can Be Victorious in Spiritual Warfare

Milton Goh

Table of Contents

Chapter 1: The First Temptation 6

Chapter 2: Satan Has No Authority Over a Believer 11

Chapter 3: The Art of Deflecting Satan's Temptations 17

Chapter 4: Shaving, Blinding and Binding Tactics 26

Chapter 5: God's People Multiply Through Satanic Persecution 30

Chapter 6: Spiritual Weapons for Destroying Satanic Strongholds .. 36

Chapter 7: Destroying the Stronghold of a Harbored Grudge 42

Chapter 8: How to Empty Yourself of Anger 48

Chapter 9: Godly Weapons that Put Satan to Flight 52

Chapter 10: Stand Firmly Upon your Gift of Righteousness 55

Chapter 11: Attack with the Sword of the Spirit 59

Chapter 12: How to Protect your Finances from the Devourer 63

Chapter 13: Understand How the Word of your Testimony is a Weapon 67

Chapter 14: Lavish Angelic Protection Against your Demonic Enemies 72

Chapter 15: It is Dangerous to Intentionally Harm God's People 77

Chapter 16: Purify your Faith for Breakthroughs by Hearing the Gospel 82

Chapter 17: The Anointing Oil Breaks Satanic Yokes 86

Chapter 18: Your God is Stronger than the Giants 91

Chapter 19: The Sting of Death is Gone 98

Chapter 20: The Value of the Blood of Jesus 102

Chapter 21: God's Love, Not your Love 107

Chapter 22: Actively Remain in your Safe Fortress 111

Chapter 23: Praying with Authority, not Timidity 117

Chapter 24: Satan Has Been Stripped of the Power of Death 121

Chapter 25: How God's Word Becomes Inoperative in a Believer's Life 126

Chapter 26: Let Go and Follow the Holy Spirit 132

Chapter 27: Purify your Faith Through Fasting 135

Chapter 28: Look Beyond the Stone 141

Chapter 29: Be Careful How You Hear 145

Chapter 30: What Satan Says About you Does Not Matter 149

Chapter 31: Be Strong in the Lord, Not in the Flesh 153

Chapter 32: Gird Up your Loins with the Truth 157

Chapter 33: Guard your Heart with the Breastplate of Righteousness 160

Chapter 34: Go Further Safely with the Gospel of Peace 163

Chapter 35: How to Use the Shield of the Faith 166

Chapter 36: Wear Hope like a Helmet 169

Chapter 37: Prayer—The Final Piece of the Whole Armor of God 172

Chapter 38: You are Blessed—Satan Cannot Curse You 176

Parting Words 180

Chapter 1: The First Temptation

"Now the serpent was more subtle than any animal of the field which Yahweh God had made. He said to the woman, "Has God really said, 'You shall not eat of any tree of the garden?'" The woman said to the serpent, "We may eat fruit from the trees of the garden, but not the fruit of the tree which is in the middle of the garden. God has said, 'You shall not eat of it. You shall not touch it, lest you die.'" The serpent said to the woman, "You won't surely die, for God knows that in the day you eat it, your eyes will be opened, and you will be like God, knowing good and evil." When the woman saw that the tree was good for food, and that it was a delight to the eyes, and that the tree was to be desired to make one wise, she took some of its fruit, and ate; and she gave some to her husband with her, and he ate it, too." (Genesis 3:1-6 WEB)

The cravings of the sinful flesh, the whisperings of demons, the voices of the world. These are all voices of the "serpent". When there are so many voices competing to have our attention, how can we focus on the still, small voice of the Holy Spirit? How can we even tell them apart? In this book, the Holy Spirit is going to teach us to get good at this!

By studying the first time Satan tempted a human, we can learn a lot about his tactics.

He possessed a serpent and tempted Eve using that disguise. Notice the kind of animal Satan chose as his host. The word translated as "subtle" is the Hebrew word "arum" which means crafty or cunning.

The way Satan tempts is very cunning. Just by subtly tweaking the truth, the lie can be very convincing.

He retains key words of the truth, but he adds deceptions to it, so that it still resembles the real thing.

When Satan tempted Eve, he started by planting seeds of doubt. "Has God really said..."

After all, Eve was absent when God talked to Adam about the tree of the knowledge of good and evil.

"Yahweh God commanded the man, saying, "You may freely eat of every tree of the garden; but you shall not eat of the tree of the knowledge of good and evil; for in the day that you eat of it, you will surely die.""" (Genesis 2:16-17 WEB)

Compare what God said to Adam with what Eve thought God said.

God never said that they would die if they touched the tree or its fruit.

This is Satan's second technique used in the first temptation: he used Eve's ignorance of God's word against her.

Many believers do not know what God's word actually says. They only hear bits and pieces from third-party sources. This makes them susceptible to falling for Satan's deceptions.

Thirdly, the place where Satan tempted Eve at is probably the tree of the knowledge of good and evil.

When people go to places of temptation, they put themselves at higher risk of falling to temptation. They longer they linger, the more opportunities demons have to convince them into sinning just 'this once' and that 'a little fun will not cause any harm'.

Lastly, Satan tried to make God appear stingy or reluctant to give Eve good things. He accused God of not wanting Adam and Eve to become like God.

Some believers today have been taught that God does not bless people with healing or prosperity. Certain preachers make God seem so angry, always cursing people for their sins and withholding good things.

These teach that there are only spiritual blessings like forgiveness of sins, but no tangible blessings.

Satan's goal is to cause people to doubt God's love and goodness, so that following God's ways seems to lead to a restricted and unhappy life, whereas giving in to the sinful cravings of the flesh produces true, abundant life.

"Don't love the world or the things that are in the world. If anyone loves the world, the Father's love isn't in him. For all that is in the world, the lust of the flesh, the lust of the eyes, and the pride of life, isn't the Father's, but is the world's." (1 John 2:15-16 WEB)

Did you realize that Satan used the three things mentioned in the passage above? Eve saw that the tree was good for food—that is the lust of the flesh. She saw that the tree was a delight to the eyes—the lust of the eyes. Then, Eve thought that the tree was desirable because it would make her wise—the pride of life.

These three types of temptation successfully caused Eve to feel separated from the God's love and to place her trust in the world instead of God.

Why did Satan want to tempt Adam and Eve? He stood to gain from it. By listening to him, Adam abdicated his position of rulership over the earth and gave it to Satan.

Satan took advantage of God's commandment to bring death into the world through sin (a transgression of God's commandment).

How does he still do this today? By deceiving Christians to keep the Law of Moses. Sin derives the power of death from the Law. Whoever breaks the Law faces the penalty of death—if there was no Law, there would be no penalty because there is no transgression.

"The sting of death is sin, and the power of sin is the law." (1 Corinthians 15:56 WEB)

Do you see how cunning Satan, the ancient serpent, is? He wields what is holy to become his weapon to inflict death. Dressing his deceptions in religious garbs, they become concealed weapons, which people thrust themselves upon, thinking they are doing what is right.

There is so much to learn, even from the first temptation. I hope you are excited, just as I look forward to sharing more ways to silence the serpent, in the chapters ahead!

Chapter 2: Satan Has No Authority Over a Believer

"Now on the day when God's sons came to present themselves before Yahweh, Satan also came among them. Yahweh said to Satan, "Where have you come from?" Then Satan answered Yahweh, and said, "From going back and forth in the earth, and from walking up and down in it."" (Job 1:6-7 WEB)

To silence the voice of the serpent, you must first understand that he has no authority over you.

Some believers have this misunderstanding that Satan has great power and authority.

Comparing based on raw strength, Satan may be more powerful than humans because of his angelic abilities, but he has no authority over a born-again believer.

Although the passage above shows Satan in God's presence, that was only in the past, before Jesus' finished work at the cross.

By successfully tempting Adam, Satan legally took over the position of ruler over the earth. Ever since then, until Jesus' ascension to Heaven, Satan had authority over the earth. We see that this true when Satan tried to tempt Jesus.

"The devil, leading him up on a high mountain, showed him all the kingdoms of the world in a moment of time. The devil said to him, 'I will give you all this authority, and their glory, for it has been delivered to me; and I give it to whomever I want. If you therefore will worship before me, it will all be yours.'" (Luke 4:5-7 WEB)

The kingdoms of the world were in Satan's power and possession. This was true at that time.
However, look at what happened after the cross.

"According to the law, nearly everything is cleansed with blood, and apart from shedding of blood there is no remission. It was necessary therefore that the copies of the things in the heavens should be cleansed with these; but the heavenly things themselves with better sacrifices than these." (Hebrews 9:22-23 WEB)

What heavenly things needed to be cleansed with the blood of Jesus? It must be referring to the place originally belonging to Adam where Satan accused the saints day and night from.
Jesus' blood has righteously reclaimed the rulership position that Adam lost. Jesus is our Kinsman Redeemer who bought

back the forfeited inheritance that mankind could not afford, and who redeemed the saints from being slaves to sin.

Read the following passage about the "right of redemption". This law is a picture of how Jesus redeemed us and the earth.

""If an alien or temporary resident with you becomes rich, and your brother beside him has grown poor, and sells himself to the stranger or foreigner living among you, or to a member of the stranger's family; after he is sold he may be redeemed. One of his brothers may redeem him; or his uncle, or his uncle's son, may redeem him, or any who is a close relative to him of his family may redeem him; or if he has grown rich, he may redeem himself. He shall reckon with him who bought him from the year that he sold himself to him to the Year of Jubilee. The price of his sale shall be according to the number of years; he shall be with him according to the time of a hired servant." (Leviticus 25:47-50 WEB)

This "right of redemption" explains why Jesus had to become a Man. A kinsman redeemer has to be wealthy enough to afford the price of redemption, consenting to do it, and must be a close relative. Only a man can redeem mankind.

In this case, the price was not money, but blood. The wages of sin is death, and the sin debt of the world had to be paid in the price of shed blood—for the life of a being is in the blood.

"For the life of the flesh is in the blood; and I have given it to you on the altar to make atonement for your souls: for it is the blood that makes atonement by reason of the life." (Leviticus 17:11 WEB)

Jesus literally gave His life for us, every drop of it, and overpaid the debt because His sinless blood is the blood of God—it is worth infinitely more than our lives all put together.

Today, Satan is nothing more than an outlaw and fugitive, who is awaiting his final sentence of condemnation. He is still stubbornly filling up the cup of God's wrath against him, increasing the severity of his future torment in the lake of fire.

In the following passage, you can see the scene of Satan and his fallen angels being permanently evicted from Heaven.

"There was war in the sky. Michael and his angels made war on the dragon. The dragon and his angels made war. They didn't prevail, neither was a place found for him any more in heaven. The great dragon was thrown down, the old serpent, he who is called the devil and Satan, the deceiver of the whole world. He was thrown down to the earth, and his angels were thrown down with him. I heard a loud voice in heaven, saying, "Now the salvation, the power, and the Kingdom of our God, and the authority of his Christ has come; for the accuser of our brothers has been thrown down, who accuses them before our God day and night." (Revelation 12:7-10 WEB)

After Jesus rose from the dead, He ascended to the Father and sprinkled His blood upon the place where Satan once stood, thoroughly cleansing it from the corruption.

Dear child of God, Satan has no authority over you. He has to resort to trickery and lies because he has no righteous basis to meddle with you.

Satan is like a defeated king who refuses to relinquish his throne. He is stubbornly clinging to it and acting as if he is still in charge, but God is patiently waiting for the appointed time to finally cast him into the lake of fire.

Today, Satan has no more access Heaven, and is confined to the realms of earth and sky. He does not rule over Hell as some movies wrongly portray—he has never been to Hell. In fact, he is terribly afraid of hellfire because it is an instrument of God's judgment against sinners.

"You were made alive when you were dead in transgressions and sins, in which you once walked according to the course of this world, according to the prince of the power of the air, the spirit who now works in the children of disobedience; among whom we also all once lived in the lusts of our flesh, doing the desires of the flesh and of the mind, and were by nature children of wrath, even as the rest." (Ephesians 2:1-3 WEB)

Satan is still "the prince of the power of the air", having authority over unbelievers—those who are still slaves to sin, but he has no claim on you. You are no longer "dead in transgressions and sins" but are forever alive to God.

"who delivered us out of the power of darkness, and translated us into the Kingdom of the Son of his love; in whom we have our redemption, the forgiveness of our sins;" (Colossians 1:13-14 WEB)

You have been irreversibly delivered out of the power of darkness and translated into Christ's kingdom. You are redeemed and forgiven.

To sum it up, you do not have to fear the devil or his demons because you have authority over him, but he has no authority over you. Once you know and believe this truth, he cannot fool you anymore with his lies, and that is a good first step in silencing the serpent.

Chapter 3: The Art of Deflecting Satan's Temptations

"Jesus, full of the Holy Spirit, returned from the Jordan, and was led by the Spirit into the wilderness for forty days, being tempted by the devil. He ate nothing in those days. Afterward, when they were completed, he was hungry." (Luke 4:1-2 WEB)

What better way to learn how to silence the serpent than to see how Jesus silenced Satan?

After Jesus was baptized in the river Jordan, the Holy Spirit descended upon Him and this anointing remained with Him to supply God's miracle-working power.

The Holy Spirit led Jesus into the wilderness to be tested by Satan. God knows that Jesus is perfect and will not succumb to temptations, but Satan didn't believe it—so, he was given the opportunity to test it out and be convinced.

Some people mistakenly think that Satan only tempted Jesus three times—actually, the three temptations recorded in the Scriptures are just the final three temptations that Satan used before departing from Jesus.

Jesus and Satan were both there in the wilderness for forty days, and Satan must have used all the tactics he could imagine, trying to get Jesus to sin. You can see in the passage on the previous page that it was only after forty days that "they were completed".

One important thing to note is that Adam was only tempted once in a place where he had an abundance of food, and he was without sin in his nature. Despite all these, he fell.

On the other hand, Jesus was tempted relentlessly for forty days in a wilderness with no food. Physically, He was suffering from hunger, but He was infallible in His spirit.

It only goes to show how much better the "last Adam" is than the first Adam. Jesus became the last Adam after His resurrection because He is the first of His kind—a new type of man, whose spirit is joined with the Holy Spirit, living in a glorified body.

"When he had fasted forty days and forty nights, he was hungry afterward. The tempter came and said to him, 'If you are the Son of God, command that these stones become bread.' But he answered, 'It is written, 'Man shall

not live by bread alone, but by every word that proceeds out of the mouth of God.""" *(Matthew 4:2-4 WEB)*

If you compare the first temptation (of Eve) and the first recorded temptation of Christ, you will see a similarity in Satan's tactics.

When Satan tempted Eve, he said, "Has God really said," and when he tempted Jesus, he said, "If you are the Son of God".

What was the "if" for? To cast doubt on God's truth. Satan subtly tried to make Jesus doubt His identity and to try proving it by obeying Satan.

Satan successfully caused Eve to doubt God's words, but Jesus could not be fooled.

Was there a good reason to tempt Jesus to turn the stones into bread? Yes, Jesus was hungry. Satan observes us and designs his temptations based on what we desire most. His goal is to divert our trust in God to trust in him instead of our heart's desires.

Continue reading the passage above and you will see another similarity between the temptation of Eve and the temptation of Christ.

Satan used Eve's ignorance of God's word against her. She thought that God said whoever touches the tree and its fruit would die.

When she touched the tree and its fruit without anything happening, she probably felt that it was alright to proceed further—to actually eat the fruit.

However, Jesus has perfect knowledge of the Scriptures, for these truths come from Him. For every temptation that Satan threw at Him, Jesus deflected it by quoting God's written word.

Jesus did the same for the other two recorded temptations. He quoted God's word and Satan had no way to respond except by trying a different temptation.

"The devil, leading him up on a high mountain, showed him all the kingdoms of the world in a moment of time. The devil said to him, "I will give you all this authority, and their glory, for it has been delivered to me; and I give it to whomever I want. If you therefore will worship before me, it will all be yours." Jesus answered him, "Get behind me Satan! For it is written, 'You shall worship the Lord your God, and you shall serve him only.'" He led him to Jerusalem, and set him on the pinnacle of the temple, and said to him, "If you are the Son of God, cast yourself down from here, for it is written, 'He will put his angels in charge of you, to guard you;' and, 'On their hands they will bear you up, lest perhaps you dash your foot against a stone.'" Jesus answering, said to him, "It has been said, 'You shall not tempt the Lord your God.'" When the devil had completed every temptation, he departed from him until another time." (Luke 4:5-13 WEB)

This is great news for us because we can do what Jesus did. The first step is to fill your spirit and mind with God's word. When you are so full of His word, the indwelling Holy Spirit can bring Scriptures to your remembrance at crucial moments when you get tempted.

Confess the Scriptures that He leads you to speak in these times.

"So faith comes by hearing, and hearing by the word of God." (Romans 10:17 WEB)

The words translated "the word of God" is "rhēmatos Christou" in the original Greek.

Rhema can be defined as what God is currently saying. The Scriptures without the intervention of the Holy Spirit are the "logos" word, which is what God has said—the written Scriptures in general.

Notice that it is rhema that causes faith to come, and not logos. It is not about randomly flipping through a page full of Scriptures and confessing all of them—there is no energizing of faith in that.

The Holy Spirit will cause a certain verse or passage to float up in your spirit and highlight it so strongly to you, giving you fresh revelations about it. This is the rhema word that causes miracle-working faith to arise in your situation.

The method that the Holy Spirit uses is secondary. Sometimes He speaks directly to you from within, at other times He uses a preacher to speak truths you need to hear, and He may even lead a friend to send a text message with a verse to encourage you.

Whatever method He chooses to speak, that is the rhema word for your situation. When you believe and confess that, God's power will be released.

If you think about the three recorded temptations of Christ, you may notice that they are similar to the temptations of Eve. When Satan tempted Jesus to turn stones to bread, that is the lust of the flesh.

When Satan tempted Jesus to worship him to receive all the kingdoms of the world, that is the lust of the eyes, because he showed Jesus all those kingdoms and their glory in a moment of time, aiming to seduce Him with the appearance of riches and power.

When Satan offers something seemingly good to you, he always robs you of something more valuable if you do accept the offer.

If Jesus had worshipped Satan, mankind would be doomed to destruction forever. Jesus would also have fallen and become Satan's slave.

It is never worth it to take a Satanic shortcut because it is a sure path to destruction. Satan only comes to steal, kill, and destroy—not to give you life more abundantly.

Finally, when Satan tempted Jesus to throw Himself down from the pinnacle of the temple to prove that God's angels would protect Him, that is the pride of life.

We must be led by God and not presumptuously test Him. I once read an article about a missionary who went to a rural civilization for evangelism. He did not even manage to successfully enter the village, and got killed by the natives without resulting in any souls saved for the Lord.

This is the danger of charging ahead without being led by the Holy Spirit, sadly resulting in bodily death. If he was truly saved, he is now in Heaven, but his mortal lifetime was cut short because of acting presumptuously.

"When they had gone through the region of Phrygia and Galatia, they were forbidden by the Holy Spirit to speak the word in Asia. When they had come opposite Mysia, they tried to go into Bithynia, but the Spirit didn't allow them. Passing by Mysia, they came down to Troas. A vision appeared to Paul in the night. There was a man of Macedonia standing, begging him, and saying, "Come over into Macedonia and help us." When he had seen the vision, immediately we sought to go out to Macedonia, concluding that the Lord had called us to preach the Good News to them." (Acts 16:6-10 WEB)

There are times when the Holy Spirit forbids you from going somewhere because it will result in your harm. If you wisely obey, you will be safe. But if you stubbornly proceed, you will only suffer.

Whatever it is, to enjoy the fullness of God's protection, we have to be led by the Holy Spirit and not act upon our impulsive emotions. The Holy Spirit will lead you to avoid unnecessary danger, but if you insist, then He will not override your free will.

Despite all the warnings from the Holy Spirit, the apostle Paul still chose to go to Jerusalem—he was ready to die. He was arrested just as the Holy Spirit warned him.

"Having found disciples, we stayed there seven days. These said to Paul through the Spirit, that he should not go up to Jerusalem...As we stayed there some days, a certain prophet named Agabus came down from Judea. Coming to us, and taking Paul's belt, he bound his own feet and hands, and said, "Thus says the Holy Spirit: 'So will the Jews at Jerusalem bind the man who owns this belt, and will deliver him into the hands of the Gentiles.'" When we heard these things, both we and they of that place begged him not to go up to Jerusalem. Then Paul answered, "What are you doing, weeping and breaking my heart? For I am ready not only to be bound, but also to die at Jerusalem for the name of the Lord Jesus." When he would not be persuaded, we ceased, saying, "The Lord's will be done."" (Acts 21:4, 10-14 WEB)

Even though Paul acted against the leading of the Holy Spirit, God still used that mistake to put Paul before rulers so that he could preach the Gospel of Jesus Christ to them.

God will make all things in your life, whether good or bad, work for good!

As we can see, Satan's tactics have not changed. He still uses the lusts of the flesh, the lusts of the eyes, and the pride of life to tempt mankind. Why? Probably because these are effective—but not on Jesus.

After trying all sorts of temptations on Jesus for forty days, Satan conceded defeat and departed from Him until another time.

Every time Satan or another demon comes to tempt you, deflect them with God's rhema word and keep them leaving with their heads hanging in defeat!

Chapter 4: Shaving, Blinding and Binding Tactics

"She made him sleep on her knees; and she called for a man, and shaved off the seven locks of his head; and she began to afflict him, and his strength went from him. She said, "The Philistines are upon you, Samson!" He awoke out of his sleep, and said, "I will go out as at other times, and shake myself free." But he didn't know that Yahweh had departed from him. The Philistines laid hold on him, and put out his eyes; and they brought him down to Gaza, and bound him with fetters of brass; and he ground at the mill in the prison." (Judges 16:19-21 WEB)

The seven locks of hair on Samson's head were the secret behind Samson's supernatural strength. Cutting his hair off caused all his strength to depart.

The secret behind a Christian's strength is not his hair, but the word of God hidden in his heart.

"How can a young man keep his way pure? By living according to your word. With my whole heart, I have sought you. Don't let me wander from your commandments. I have hidden your word in my heart, that I might not sin against you." (Psalms 119:9-11 WEB)

Satan tries to cut off the secret of our strength by diverting us from God's word. He brings in all sorts of attractive distractions like Delilah into our lives to lure us away from spending time in the Scriptures.

Samson's enemies knew that his weakness was his lust for women, and they used it against him.

Satan's lackeys observe our behavior to find out what sins we are secretly practicing. When they see a weak spot, they just send temptations in that area, to make the indulgences worse.

Do you notice that when you neglect spending time in God's word, you feel lethargic, easily irritable, and more likely to give in to temptations? God's word is the secret of your strength.

The Philistines blinded Samson, weakening him even further. Even though Satan wants to physically blind every human, he cannot do that—he has to work within boundaries set by God.

Satan blinds people spiritually. Using convincing lies, he covers up the truth, causing the deceived to live defeated lives.

For example, some people believe that only their past sins are forgiven, and that all sins committed since the time they received Jesus as Lord are not forgiven—that they are now held at a higher standard of accountability because they know Jesus.

These wrong beliefs often come from hearing false teachings. As a result, believers fall into sin consciousness and the self-condemnation traps them in a vicious cycle of sin. The more they try to become righteous by their own strength, they more they are doomed to repeat their sins.

Such lies are also like fetters of brass (usually placed around the ankles), shackling believers who believe in them, affecting their walk in life.

In the Bible, brass represents judgment. Some people are chained by condemnation and regret from the past on one ankle, and trapped by fears and worries about the future on the other ankle.

It all stems from the fear of God's judgment—that they would fail or be punished because of their sins.

Satan has them paralyzed and tip toeing around like scared kittens, when they are actually fully-grown lions in Christ.

When a believer is shaved, blinded, and bound, he is hardly a threat to Satan's strongholds of darkness.

Even if you have been caught in one of Satan's traps, there is always hope.

"However the hair of his head began to grow again after he was shaved." (Judges 16:22 WEB)

God will lead you to feed on His word again. When you reconnect yourself to the secret of your strength, it is like your hair growing back.

When your hair returns, so does your strength. The single habit of feeding on true teachings of God's word restores your hair, opens blind eyes, and breaks fetters of brass.

Put God's word back in your daily walk, and schedule it for the early part of each day. When you are strong because of God's word, it is easier to silence the serpent!

Chapter 5: God's People Multiply Through Satanic Persecution

"Now there arose a new king over Egypt, who didn't know Joseph. He said to his people, "Behold, the people of the children of Israel are more and mightier than we. Come, let us deal wisely with them, lest they multiply, and it happen that when any war breaks out, they also join themselves to our enemies, and fight against us, and escape out of the land." Therefore they set taskmasters over them to afflict them with their burdens. They built storage cities for Pharaoh: Pithom and Raamses. But the more they afflicted them, the more they multiplied and the more they spread out. They were grieved because of the children of Israel. The Egyptians ruthlessly made the children of Israel serve, and they made their lives bitter with hard service, in mortar and in brick, and in all kinds of service in the field, all their service, in which they ruthlessly made them serve." (Exodus 1:8-14 WEB)

Pharaoh is a picture of Satan. He was probably directly manipulated by Satan because the children of Israel were obviously favored—Abraham, Isaac and Jacob had covenants with God and their descendants were the most likely to produce the prophesied seed of the woman who would crush the serpent's head (Genesis 3:15).

Satan knows that believers are mightier than the demons because of the authority they have received from God.

Therefore, his strategy is also to afflict believers to prevent them from multiplying and increasing in strength.

The taskmasters that Pharaoh appointed form a picture of Satan's demons. Satan sends demons to afflict believers.

If you watched the animated film "Prince of Egypt", you could see an artist's impression of how the children of Israel were whipped by Egyptian taskmasters to force them to work faster and harder.

Today, demons enforce this kind of slavery spiritually. The whippings are replaced with harsh accusations to cause self-condemnation and sin consciousness.

In place of literal hard labor, demons tempt mankind to depend on works of the flesh, advocating stressful toil to obtain good things.

Many people are tortured by guilt and burdened by the belief that no one will take care of them besides themselves. They are enslaved by wrong beliefs.

However, there is a ray of hope in the passage we read. The more Pharaoh afflicted the children of Israel, the more they multiplied and spread out.

Satan is unable to stop God's plans. God's people multiply through persecution. Every time the devil sends a wave of persecution, the church grows stronger and multiplies through it. We see this happening in the book of Acts.

"Saul was consenting to his death. A great persecution arose against the assembly which was in Jerusalem in that day. They were all scattered abroad throughout the regions of Judea and Samaria, except for the apostles. Devout men buried Stephen, and lamented greatly over him. But Saul ravaged the assembly, entering into every house, and dragged both men and women off to prison. Therefore those who were scattered abroad went around preaching the word. Philip went down to the city of Samaria, and proclaimed to them the Christ. The multitudes listened with one accord to the things that were spoken by Philip, when they heard and saw the signs which he did. For unclean spirits came out of many of those who had them. They came out, crying with a loud voice. Many who had been paralyzed and lame were healed. There was great joy in that city." (Acts 8:1-8 WEB)

When Saul (before he became the apostle Paul) persecuted the church in Jerusalem, the believers were scattered—they fled, spreading outwards and taking the Gospel of Jesus Christ to other regions such as Judea and Samaria.

Philip was mightily used by God in Samaria, and a healthy local church grew in that region from his work in the Lord.

The growth was so significant that the apostles sent Peter and John to Samaria to baptize the new believers in the Holy Spirit, and they even preached to other villages of the Samaritans on the way back.

"Now when the apostles who were at Jerusalem heard that Samaria had received the word of God, they sent Peter and John to them, who, when they had come down, prayed for them, that they might receive the Holy Spirit; for as yet he had fallen on none of them. They had only been baptized in the name of Christ Jesus. Then they laid their hands on them, and they received the Holy Spirit...They therefore, when they had testified and spoken the word of the Lord, returned to Jerusalem, and preached the Good News to many villages of the Samaritans." (Acts 8:14-17, 25 WEB)

As you can see, every time the devil persecutes God's people, it just results in great restoration for them. On the other hand, whether on a corporate or individual level, believers who do not experience persecution grow less.

There is limited growth in the comfort zone where there is limited opportunity to exercise one's faith.

Therefore, if you are facing persecution, it is a time of growth and multiplication. Get ready to expand through the experience.

If you examine how Satan and his demons afflict the saints, you may notice that they are actually wielding the Law (the Ten Commandments engraved on the two stone tablets) as a weapon.

By deceiving believers to harbor sin consciousness, self-condemnation, and reliance on the flesh for justification, those who are deceived place themselves under the Law and are afflicted by its curse.

The Law curses whoever does not keep all the Ten Commandments perfectly in both thought and deed. Something that is so holy, righteous, and true is used by Satan to afflict the ignorant with death.

Even after the children of Israel had been freed from Egypt and Pharaoh by the mighty hand of God, they still looked back fondly on their days in Egypt.

"The whole congregation of the children of Israel murmured against Moses and against Aaron in the wilderness; and the children of Israel said to them, "We wish that we had died by Yahweh's hand in the land of Egypt, when we sat by the meat pots, when we ate our fill of bread, for you have brought us out into this wilderness, to kill this whole assembly with hunger."" *(Exodus 16:2-3 WEB)*

Instead of being happy to be free men, they would have rather become slaves again just so they could have food at predictable timings. The children of Israel were essentially saying that they did not mind getting afflicted by the taskmasters and doing hard labor in exchange for food.

Just because the Ten Commandments of the Law appeals to the flesh with its naturally predictable results (do good get good, do bad get bad), does not mean that we who have become children of God should act as though we were slaves to sin.

"But when the fullness of the time came, God sent out his Son, born to a woman, born under the law, that he might redeem those who were under the law, that we might receive the adoption of children. And because you are children, God sent out the Spirit of his Son into your hearts, crying, "Abba, Father!" So you are no longer a bondservant, but a son; and if a son, then an heir of God through Christ. However at that time, not knowing God, you were in bondage to those who by nature are not gods. But now that you have come to know God, or rather to be known by God, why do you turn back again to the weak and miserable elemental principles, to which you desire to be in bondage all over again?" (Galatians 4:4-9 WEB)

Dear child of God, trying to justify yourself by obeying the Ten Commandments is like enslaving yourself to Pharaoh. It is subjecting yourself to be afflicted with severe bondage.

You have been redeemed from the Law and are now an heir of God, thanks to Jesus' finished work at the cross. Just remember, you are a precious son, not an unloved slave!

Chapter 6: Spiritual Weapons for Destroying Satanic Strongholds

"For though we walk in the flesh, we don't wage war according to the flesh; for the weapons of our warfare are not of the flesh, but mighty before God to the throwing down of strongholds, throwing down imaginations and every high thing that is exalted against the knowledge of God, and bringing every thought into captivity to the obedience of Christ;" (2 Corinthians 10:3-5 WEB)

Although we are spirits living in a body of flesh, we do not fight our battles against Satan with fleshly weapons.

We have access to much more powerful weapons which are spiritual, not physical.

Spiritual weapons are far stronger because it is the eternal Spirit that created the temporal physical world. God (spirit) spoke and created the heavens and the earth (physical).

Satan sets up strongholds not at a geographical location, but inside a person's mind. Notice how the passage used language referring to the mind: "imaginations", "knowledge" and "thought".

A stronghold (in Greek: ochuróma) is a heavily fortified, strong-walled fortress. If a physical stronghold is built with bricks, the Satanic equivalent of a brick is a thought.

A Satanic stronghold is not built overnight, but rather an accumulation of many wrong thoughts used to justify a wrong belief.

The person who has a Satanic stronghold set up in his mind is like a prisoner trapped inside.

The words "throwing down" (in Greek: kathairesis) means to destroy or demolish, like using a catapult throwing flaming boulders to destroy the stronghold.

The words "high thing" in the passage are referring to things like walls and ramparts which surround the stronghold.

The spiritual weapons we have access to are able to destroy every layer of the enemy's fortifications and free the prisoners within.

After destroying the enemy's stronghold, the remaining wrong thoughts are "brought into captivity" like prisoners of war.

What is the force attacking the Satanic stronghold? The answer is found in the last line of the passage—the obedience of Christ.

"And being found in human form, he humbled himself, becoming obedient to death, yes, the death of the cross." (Philippians 2:8 WEB)

In other words, the obedience of Christ refers to Jesus' finished work at the cross—the central focus of the Gospel.

Every Satanic stronghold can be obliterated by receiving a fresh revelation of the obedience of Christ.

Are you experiencing a sickness and think that you are going to live with it for the rest of your life? Maybe many negative thoughts have accumulated and made you believe that the condition is incurable.

"But he was pierced for our transgressions. He was crushed for our iniquities. The punishment that brought our peace was on him; and by his wounds we are healed." (Isaiah 53:5 WEB)

See the lash wounds on Jesus' body and picture Him bearing all your sicknesses in His body at the cross. He already paid the full price for your healing. This is how the "obedience of Christ" can demolition a Satanic stronghold about sickness.

Or perhaps you are facing some financial stress and thinking that other people may be wealthy, but you are always going to be in lack.

"For you know the grace of our Lord Jesus Christ, that, though he was rich, yet for your sakes he became poor, that you through his poverty might become rich." (2 Corinthians 8:9 WEB)

Visualize how Jesus became poor at the cross—He is the richest King in existence and yet He willingly hung there stark naked and penniless, like a worthless criminal so that we could inherit all His riches.

The cross had made you as righteous as God, so every blessing is yours to receive freely—material provision is one of them. We are children of God, and our Father wants us to prosper in all things, and be healthy, even as our souls prosper (3 John 1:2)

Through a revelation of the "obedience of Christ" from this perspective, a Satanic stronghold about poverty can be destroyed.

Do you have secret sinful habits that you practice such as porn addiction or substance abuse? These bondages can feel like a stronghold which you cannot escape from.

"In this love has been made perfect among us, that we may have boldness in the day of judgment, because as he is, even so are we in this world." (1 John 4:17 WEB)

Meditate on how Jesus' finished work at the cross has perfectly cleansed you of your sins such that you are holy, righteous, and perfect just as Jesus is right now in Heaven.

The problem with sinful habits is that the resulting shame and guilt traps you into repeating those sins. If you think that you are dirty, pathetic, and hopeless, there is no way to climb out of a mire of sin.

On the other hand, if you have a fresh revelation of how clean you have become in Christ, your spirit will be empowered to bring the sinful flesh into submission—the fruit of self-control will manifest, and you will desire to do what pleases God.

Just like that, a Satanic stronghold about addiction can be destroyed.

"For I am not ashamed of the Good News of Christ, for it is the power of God for salvation for everyone who believes; for the Jew first, and also for the Greek." (Romans 1:16 WEB)

The word "power" in the verse above is "dunamis" in Greek, which often refers to the miracle-working power of God. The word "dynamite" comes from this same word.

If you are trapped by a Satanic stronghold, you cannot reason or will your way out of it, for those are fleshly weapons of the soul (mind, will and emotions).

You cannot defeat Satan with fleshly weapons—he has had thousands of years to refine and improve the effectiveness of his tactics. However, Satan has no defence against the Gospel.

You need a white-hot revelation of the Gospel of Jesus Christ, just like lighting up a dynamite. Look out, the accompanying explosion of God's power is going to set you free!

Chapter 7: Destroying the Stronghold of a Harbored Grudge

"This punishment which was inflicted by the many is sufficient for such a one; so that on the contrary you should rather forgive him and comfort him, lest by any means such a one should be swallowed up with his excessive sorrow. Therefore I beg you to confirm your love toward him. For to this end I also wrote, that I might know the proof of you, whether you are obedient in all things. Now I also forgive whomever you forgive anything. For if indeed I have forgiven anything, I have forgiven that one for your sakes in the presence of Christ, that no advantage may be gained over us by Satan; for we are not ignorant of his schemes." (2 Corinthians 2:6-11 WEB)

Among the Corinthian church, there was a man who was having sexual relations with his stepmother. In the apostle Paul's first letter to the Corinthians, he instructed them to exile that man as a punishment.

However, after he had been dealt sufficient punishment, Paul wrote to the Corinthian church in his second letter (as seen in the passage in the previous page) to forgive this man and receive him back as a brother.

In the last sentence, Paul implied that the unwillingness to forgive a person and harboring a grudge gives Satan an advantage and is one of his schemes.

This is just one of many ways that Satan gets an advantage, but it is significant enough for Paul to write that by the Spirit.

"looking carefully lest there be any man who falls short of the grace of God; lest any root of bitterness springing up trouble you, and many be defiled by it;" (Hebrews 12:15 WEB)

The unwillingness to forgive a person is a seed that becomes a root of bitterness, bringing trouble and defilement—not just to one person, but to many.

How does this become a stronghold? When a person is harboring a grudge, every little thing the other person does seems to be annoying and offensive. These 'faults' become the bricks that build the stronghold of a harbored grudge.

Other excuses like, "I cannot forgive him so easily, I must teach him a lesson. If not, he will never change his ways," further reinforce the stronghold. Since when do fleshly efforts ever successfully reform a person from within? On top of that, it is not punishment, but rather grace, that produces true repentance.

The reason for us to forgive others is not because they have changed or that they said sorry for what they did to hurt you. It should have nothing to do with them earning forgiveness.

Once again, we have to throw the flaming boulders of the "obedience of Christ" to demolish this stronghold.

How did you receive forgiveness of sins from God? Did you earn it by being good enough? Did you sincerely change your ways and stop sinning for the rest of your life?

No, you received forgiveness of sins by God's Grace. It is His gift of unmerited favor towards you.

"Therefore the Kingdom of Heaven is like a certain king, who wanted to reconcile accounts with his servants. When he had begun to reconcile, one was brought to him who owed him ten thousand talents. But because he couldn't pay, his lord commanded him to be sold, with his wife, his children, and all that he had, and payment to be made. The servant therefore fell down and knelt before him, saying, 'Lord, have patience with me, and I will repay you all!' The lord of that servant, being moved with compassion, released him, and forgave him the debt. "But that servant went out, and found one of his fellow servants, who owed him one hundred denarii, and he grabbed him, and took him by the throat, saying, 'Pay me what you owe!' "So his fellow servant fell down at his feet and begged him, saying, 'Have

patience with me, and I will repay you!' He would not, but went and cast him into prison, until he should pay back that which was due. So when his fellow servants saw what was done, they were exceedingly sorry, and came and told to their lord all that was done. Then his lord called him in, and said to him, 'You wicked servant! I forgave you all that debt, because you begged me. Shouldn't you also have had mercy on your fellow servant, even as I had mercy on you?'" (Matthew 18:23-33 WEB)

Since Jesus did not specifically say whether the currency was gold or silver, let us use gold as an example. Jesus compared our sin debt which we owed God to the ten thousand talents of gold. Based on the gold price today, that would be worth about $20 billion.

Jesus then compared the debt others owe us to one hundred denarii of gold which is worth only about $28,000 today.

Therefore, to put things in the correct perspective, your lifetime of sins against God is far more severe than whatever way anyone can sin against you. This is because you sin against God every day, and you are committing this crime against the King of Heaven and earth. To commit a crime against a monarch is deserving of death—what more if you keep doing it daily without turning from your ways.

If you just focus on how God has already forgiven you of a debt you could never repay, you will be empowered to extend forgiveness to fellow men.

In contrast to how you sinned against God, what people did wrong to you is negligible.

"Therefore I tell you, her sins, which are many, are forgiven, for she loved much. But to whom little is forgiven, the same loves little."" (Luke 7:47 WEB)

When you have a fresh revelation of the immensity of what God has forgiven you of, you can manifest your love for Him through forgiving others of their debts against you.

You are extending forgiveness by Grace for God's sake, not because the other person has made amends.

Knowing how much God has forgiven you of through Jesus' finished work at the cross is the flaming boulder packed full of God's dunamis (miracle-working power) to destroy the stronghold of a harbored grudge.

Harboring a grudge is like a poison that only harms yourself and others. The only ones celebrating over your unwillingness to forgive are Satan and his demons. The root of bitterness in your heart must be destroyed before it causes more trouble and defilement.

If you are harboring a grudge against someone, go through this process:

1) Meditate on the truths shared in this chapter, focusing on how God has already forgiven you of a debt that is infinitely greater than what that person owes you.

2) Identify the person by name and tell God that you are going to forgive him or her by Grace, for Jesus' sake.

3) Pray a blessing for that person and ask God to orchestrate opportunities for him or her to receive salvation through faith in Jesus Christ. This way, you overcome evil with good.

4) Congratulations, you are free from that grudge. Now that you have released the person from guilt, you also freed yourself from the stronghold of a harbored grudge. Enjoy that freedom and do not take that grudge back again!

Chapter 8: How to Empty Yourself of Anger

"BE ANGRY [at sin—at immorality, at injustice, at ungodly behavior], YET DO NOT SIN; do not let your anger [cause you shame, nor allow it to] last until the sun goes down. And do not give the devil an opportunity [to lead you into sin by holding a grudge, or nurturing anger, or harboring resentment, or cultivating bitterness]." (Ephesians 4:26-27 AMP)

It is not a sin to be angry. It is written in the Scriptures that God has anger and wrath against sin. If being angry was a sin, God would have sinned.

Being angry is not sinful, but the emotion of anger tends to cloud our better judgment and drive us to make poor decisions.

It is far easier to make good decisions when you are at peace.

We get angry at times, there is no condemnation for it, but it is crucial that we find a healthy outlet to release that anger before we go to sleep.

Pent up anger is toxic to the body and soul. When it festers, it also produces a root of bitterness, which we learnt causes trouble and defilement to many.

Anger is linked to the previous chapter about harboring grudges because it begins with anger, and unresolved anger becomes a harbored grudge.

Satan wants you to nurture that anger because it gives him many opportunities to wreak havoc in your life. He can easily convince you to sin when you hold on to that anger.

The world has some tips for reducing anger, such as deep breathing. This is effective to some extent, but if you are not thinking rationally, it is hard to remember to do it.

A more permanent solution is offered in the verses that Paul wrote before discussing anger. Paul never gave an instruction to do something before teaching how it can be done.

"if indeed you heard him, and were taught in him, even as truth is in Jesus: that you put away, as concerning your former way of life, the old man, that grows corrupt after the lusts of deceit; and that you be renewed in the spirit of your mind, and put on the new man, who in the likeness of God has been created in righteousness and holiness of truth." (Ephesians 4:21-24 WEB)

We are spirit beings who have a soul and live in a body. The spirit is the true you.

The "old man" refers to your old human spirit which was in the likeness of Adam. It was dead because of sin and crucified together with Jesus at the cross when you placed your faith in Him.

The "new man" is your born-again human spirit that has joined with the Holy Spirit. It is forever alive to God, and permanently righteous, holy, and perfect.

We have to "put away" the old man in our minds because our soul (mind, will and emotions) and body have not been regenerated yet. They are still tainted by sin.

The soul has to be progressively renewed by receiving God's word, and our bodies will only be free from sin in the flesh when we receive our glorified bodies from the Lord when He returns for us.

Most new believers have no idea what Jesus' finished work at the cross has accomplished for them. This is something we learn as we keep hearing more and more messages being preached.

Therefore, it is no surprise that new believers still think that the sinful flesh and its impulses are the real them. They obey the desires of the flesh because they do not understand their new identity in Christ.

Satan takes advantage of that ignorance and deceives believers into thinking that the impulses of the flesh are from their true selves. He heaps accusations and condemnation when they act on those impulses.

However, the more you hear about Jesus, and what His finished work at the cross has accomplished for you, the more your progressively renewed mind will see the righteous reborn spirit as the real you.

Once you reach the point of seeing your sinful flesh as a separate entity from your true self, that disassociation will help you to conquer the flesh's tendencies towards anger.

When the flesh gets angry, take authority over it, and bring it to submission. There is no absolutely right way to do it, but you could say, "In Christ, my spirit is full of shalom peace. Let that peace manifest in my mind, emotions, and body right now in Jesus' name. Amen!"

That is how you dispel the emotion of anger from the inside out. Keep feeding on messages about who you are and what you have in Christ. It will get easier to take authority over your flesh and bring it to submission.

Chapter 9: Godly Weapons that Put Satan to Flight

"They overcame him because of the Lamb's blood, and because of the word of their testimony. They didn't love their life, even to death." (Revelation 12:11 WEB)

You cannot silence Satan the ancient serpent by your willpower. Logical reasonings will not make him leave you alone.

Emotional outbursts of loud shouting or screaming will only make him laugh in glee.

Swords and arrows cannot destroy Satan either because he is a spirit.

As we previously examined, carnal weapons are ineffective against him and the strongholds he sets up.

However, God has given us spiritual weapons to overcome Satan. Satan has no defence against the holy blood of Jesus and the word of our testimony about Jesus.

"Be subject therefore to God. But resist the devil, and he will flee from you." (James 4:7 WEB)

The Holy Spirit once taught me that Satan flees when you resist Him with God's spiritual weapons because he feels intense pain, like the sensation of being burnt by hellfire (God designed that fire for punishing Satan).

"And take the helmet of salvation, and the sword of the Spirit, which is the word of God;" (Ephesians 6:17 WEB)

The apostle Paul wrote that the spoken word (rhema) of God is the sword of the Spirit. Confessing God's word is certainly powerful enough to fend off Satan and send him running off while howling in pain.

How to resist Satan? For example, when he comes against you with the lie that you will never be healed from your sickness, you can declare that by the blood of Jesus and by the testimony of God's word that says "by His stripes you are healed", you will surely be healed.

It is similar to how Jesus deflected Satan's temptations in the wilderness by quoting God's word. Satan eventually fled. Jesus did not need to declare the blood of Jesus because He is always sinless and righteous.

When you resist Satan this way, he will be smitten by God's power. Satan and his demons may resist for a while, but if you persist, they will eventually give up and flee.

Fleeing means escaping urgently in haste. If there was no pain involved, why would the devil run away? He could just reluctantly take his time to walk away.

Spirits can definitely feel pain, and I believe they feel it at a much higher intensity than us in our limited mortal bodies. If not, how will the lake of fire be an eternal torment for Satan and the fallen angels?

Satan and his demons have free choice like we do. This means that they can choose their targets for temptation. If you are always quoting God's word against them and confessing the blood of Jesus to harm them, you will gain a reputation of being feared among the demonic circles. I think they will choose to skip over your name!

Chapter 10: Stand Firmly Upon your Gift of Righteousness

"Therefore put on the whole armor of God, that you may be able to withstand in the evil day, and, having done all, to stand. Stand therefore, having the utility belt of truth buckled around your waist, and having put on the breastplate of righteousness," (Ephesians 6:13-14)

If you are a born-again Christian, Satan and his demons know it because you have a mark of God on your forehead that is visible in the spirit.

Satan knows that you are already righteous in Christ and that you do not need to struggle to receive any blessings.

However, his scheme is to move you away from relying on the gift of righteousness, to performing works for righteousness.

He wants you to frustrate the grace of God and nullify what Jesus did for you by tricking you to earn your righteousness. If you attempt to become justified through works, you come under the curse of the Law. It is like a homing missile locking on to you once you switch to 'works-based justification mode'.

The apostle Paul told us to stand. You already have the gift of righteousness through faith in Jesus Christ, so stand firmly on this truth.

This knowledge of righteousness by faith is like a breastplate that guards your heart from Satan's fiery darts of lies and intimidation. You become resistant to fear and worries when you believe that you are irrevocably righteous by faith.

Do not let Satan trick you into moving away from the foundation of faith in Jesus' finished work at the cross, because that is your only basis for receiving every one of God's blessings.

Satan will say anything to get you chasing something else for your righteousness. Here are some hypothetical examples of his lies:

"You haven't prayed long and hard enough. Others are on their knees praying and you are here playing games? What a disgrace!"

"You haven't tried fasting to get blessings. Look at that faithful man who fasted forty days! And what are you doing? Sitting here on the couch and eating potato chips? No wonder you're not blessed!"

"You are ignorant about God's word. You need to read the whole Bible first before God will bless you. Why are you reading this gossip rubbish online? If you were really righteous, you wouldn't even want to do this."

Satan is an expert at mixing in some truth with some lies. It sounds very convincing to the flesh, but the condemnation and attempts at earning righteousness result in a defeated Christian.

When you start thinking this way, "I must do more of (blank) so that God will bless me with (blank)," you have unconsciously come under works-based justification which places you under the curse of the Law.

Sure, praying, fasting, and reading God's word are wonderful and good, but not if you are trying to use them to become more righteous before God so that you can be blessed. These spiritual activities are ways for us to enter the state of faith without unbelief, so that we can receive God's blessings through faith.

The more we hear the good news of Jesus Christ, the more we will want to talk to God (pray), become more sensitive to His Spirit through fasting, and know who we are and what we have in Christ by reading and hearing God's word.

"For if by the trespass of the one, death reigned through the one; so much more will those who receive the abundance of grace and of the gift of righteousness reign in life through the one, Jesus Christ." (Romans 5:17 WEB)

You already have the gift of righteousness and God's grace is constantly being supplied into your life. Stand on this firm foundation and do not let Satan trick you into abandoning this priceless treasure that you have received.

When Satan tries to accuse you of something so that you feel unrighteous, you can confidently declare that you are righteous by faith, not by works!

Chapter 11: Attack with the Sword of the Spirit

"Put on the whole armor of God, that you may be able to stand against the wiles of the devil." (Ephesians 6:11 WEB)

The "whole armor" in Greek is panoplía (from pás, "every" and hóplon, "weapon"), meaning a complete set of defensive and offensive armor (weapons), i.e. everything needed to wage successful warfare.

It refers to the full resources the Lord gives to believers so they can successfully wage spiritual warfare. In this way they do not fight for victory—but from His victory!

I dislike how some films portray Satan and his demons to be so powerful, able to throw Christians around and kill them easily. This is fiction, designed to induce fear in those who do not know God's word.

God has not left us helpless in this world. We do not fight against flesh and blood, but against demonic spirits.

We have received both offensive and defensive spiritual weapons from God. We can attack, and we can defend. We will just focus on the offensive weapons for this chapter.

Did you ever kill a bug by crushing it quickly between two hands? In a celebratory context, we call that clapping. But when that seemingly harmless act is applied to a bug, it results in death.

That is the power of God's word. When He releases it lightly, it is like letting a bug rest on your finger. When He unleashes a greater intensity of His word, it becomes a sword of the Spirit that destroys the wicked.

"For as the rain comes down and the snow from the sky, and doesn't return there, but waters the earth, and makes it grow and bud, and gives seed to the sower and bread to the eater; so is my word that goes out of my mouth: it will not return to me void, but it will accomplish that which I please, and it will prosper in the thing I sent it to do." (Isaiah 55:10-11 WEB)

When God releases His word gently like rain and snow, it results in life. He uses His word lovingly towards us, to cause us to prosper.

""Isn't my word like fire?" says Yahweh; "and like a hammer that breaks the rock in pieces?" (Jeremiah 23:29 WEB)

But if He turns up the intensity of His word and sends a flood, all living beings on land were killed (as seen in the flood during the days of Noah).

No wonder Jesus does not need to hold any weapons to defeat the Antichrist. His spoken word is powerful enough like a sharp, double-edged sword. One word spoken with killing intent is like a beam of laser, obliterating all sinful flesh.

"Out of his mouth proceeds a sharp, double-edged sword, that with it he should strike the nations. He will rule them with an iron rod. He treads the wine press of the fierceness of the wrath of God, the Almighty...The rest were killed with the sword of him who sat on the horse, the sword which came out of his mouth. All the birds were filled with their flesh." (Revelation 19:15, 21 WEB)

You are using this powerful sword of the Spirit when you speak God's word (in Greek: rhema, meaning the spoken word). Do not despise the simple act of confessing Scriptures by faith—it obliterates Satanic strongholds, sending Satan and his demons fleeing in terror.

"And take the helmet of salvation, and the sword of the Spirit, which is the word of God; with all prayer and requests, praying at all times in the Spirit, and being watchful to this end in all perseverance and requests for all the saints:" (Ephesians 6:17-18 WEB)

The word translated as "with" in the verse above is "dia" in Greek which should actually be "through".

If you want to use the sword of the Spirit precisely, then do it through praying in tongues (it is the same thing as praying in the Spirit). Let the Holy Spirit direct the sword to cut like a master swordsman. No demonic enemy can stay hidden or defend against this weapon!

Chapter 12: How to Protect your Finances from the Devourer

"You have sown much, and bring in little. You eat, but you don't have enough. You drink, but you aren't filled with drink. You clothe yourselves, but no one is warm, and he who earns wages earns wages to put them into a bag with holes in it."" *(Haggai 1:6 WEB)*

The word "tithe" means a tenth (or ten percent). Believers who do not give tithes struggle with lack of provision and do not see much favor in their career, business, and investments.

This kind of lack is like when they receive their income, invariably money is lost by paying doctor bills, miscellaneous fees due to unforeseen damages, etc. It is similar to putting your wages in a bag full of holes.

They try to make up for the loss with stressful labor—putting in extra hours and pushing their bodies to the limit, harming their health. When these hardships happen, they blame God and question where the provision is.

Besides being a form of worship and thanksgiving towards God, tithing is also an act of sowing seeds for a harvest.

"Now may he who supplies seed to the sower and bread for food, supply and multiply your seed for sowing, and increase the fruits of your righteousness; you being enriched in everything to all liberality, which produces through us thanksgiving to God." (2 Corinthians 9:10-11 WEB)

Satan can try to deceive you into not tithing to deprive you of God's blessing, but once you tithe, Satan has no power to stop the blessing from happening.

"Bring the whole tithe into the storehouse, that there may be food in my house, and test me now in this," says Yahweh of Armies, "if I will not open you the windows of heaven, and pour you out a blessing, that there will not be room enough for. I will rebuke the devourer for your sakes, and he shall not destroy the fruits of your ground; neither shall your vine cast its fruit before its time in the field," says Yahweh of Armies. "All nations shall call you blessed, for you will be a delightful land," says Yahweh of Armies." (Malachi 3:10-12 WEB)

God Himself asks you to test Him in tithing, and He promises to pour out an abundant blessing for you—much more than you give.

God also promises to rebuke the devourer for your sake. The literal devourer is a locust or any crop-eating pest, but it is a picture of Satan.

"Be sober and self-controlled. Be watchful. Your adversary, the devil, walks around like a roaring lion, seeking whom he may devour." (1 Peter 5:8 WEB)

When you tithe, Satan cannot devour you—he has to look for another prey.

The "fruit of your ground" and "your vine in the field" represent your livelihood—your savings, career, business, and investments. All these are guaranteed God's protection when you tithe.

When you tithe, you will experience the blessedness of sealing the holes in your money bag and reaping bigger harvests with low effort.

The tithe results in enjoyment of God's unmerited favor in the area of your finances, without the need for stressful labor.

You may be wondering, "Is the passage in Malachi really talking about financial blessing or is it spiritual blessing?"

The answer is that it is a spiritual blessing that will manifest visibly, such that "all nations shall call you blessed"—they will see the physical evidence of God's blessing in your life.

Under the New Covenant of Grace, abstaining from tithing does not cause you to be under a curse, since Jesus already redeemed you from the curse.

"While the earth remains, seed time and harvest, and cold and heat, and summer and winter, and day and night will not cease."'" (Genesis 8:22 WEB)

However, the principle of sowing and reaping (seed time and harvest) will continue as long as this earth endures. If you want to receive a harvest, you must sow in good ground—and Jesus' finished work at the cross makes your sowing produce fruitful results.

If there seems to be many holes in your money bag, check whether you are tithing. This is the best way to increase and secure your finances.

You do not need to attend motivational seminars by the world's so-called experts to solve your financial problems. Allow God to make you prosper, the restful way!

Chapter 13: Understand How the Word of your Testimony is a Weapon

"Then David said to the Philistine, "You come to me with a sword, with a spear, and with a javelin; but I come to you in the name of Yahweh of Armies, the God of the armies of Israel, whom you have defied. Today, Yahweh will deliver you into my hand. I will strike you, and take your head from off you. I will give the dead bodies of the army of the Philistines today to the birds of the sky, and to the wild animals of the earth; that all the earth may know that there is a God in Israel, and that all this assembly may know that Yahweh doesn't save with sword and spear; for the battle is Yahweh's, and he will give you into our hand.""" (1 Samuel 17:45-47 WEB)

Goliath came in full heavy armor with a big sword, spear, and javelin, but David defeated him with only a sling and a small stone. It is not about the size of your carnal weapons. Spiritual weapons are far more powerful.

David came against Goliath "in the name of Yahweh". That was his main weapon—not the sling and stone. The word of his testimony (about Yahweh) was his spiritual weapon to overcome the agent of Satan.

Look how David operated this weapon. He spoke and declared what he believed Yahweh would do for him. His spoken words gave God the consent to show Himself strong in David's life. Everything that David said came true.

What are you saying about Jesus? That is the word of your testimony that has the power to overcome Satan.

"They overcame him because of the Lamb's blood, and because of the word of their testimony. They didn't love their life, even to death." (Revelation 12:11 WEB)

When faced with the giant of sickness, are you going to say that the sickness will kill you, or that the sickness has to leave your body because Jesus has already paid for your healing at the cross?

If you are up against the giant of depression, are you declaring that you will spiral downwards and go insane, or that Jesus' head was pierced by the crown of thorns to give you a sound mind?

What you speak has power to result in either life or death.

Satan wants to use this weapon of the "word of testimony" to cause havoc. When he recruits witches and occultists to serve him, he uses the word of their testimony to cast curses and hexes upon people and cities.

Humans have this great spiritual power in their tongue, but unbelievers have less power in their words than believers do.

"Most certainly I tell you, he who believes in me, the works that I do, he will do also; and he will do greater works than these, because I am going to my Father. Whatever you will ask in my name, that will I do, that the Father may be glorified in the Son. If you will ask anything in my name, I will do it." (John 14:12-14 WEB)

Jesus said that we will receive whatever we ask for in His name, but unbelievers have no such promise.

Long before David killed Goliath, he had already been trained by God for that victory.

"David said to Saul, "Your servant was keeping his father's sheep; and when a lion or a bear came, and took a lamb out of the flock, I went out after him, and struck him, and rescued it out of his mouth. When he arose against me, I caught him by his beard, and struck him, and killed him. Your servant struck both the lion and the bear. This uncircumcised Philistine shall be as one of them, since he has defied the armies of the living God." David said, "Yahweh who delivered me out of the paw of the lion,

and out of the paw of the bear, he will deliver me out of the hand of this Philistine." Saul said to David, "Go! Yahweh will be with you."" (1 Samuel 17:34-37 WEB)

The lion and the bear represent challenges that David overcame in the past. Goliath was a greater enemy, but David was not afraid because the Lord had showed Himself faithful and strong on previous occasions.

Sometimes, God allows you to go through challenges in life that He knows you can endure. God is not sending you to your doom but allowing you to have an opportunity to claim a victory. You will be prepared and strengthened for greater victories to come.

Think back on the challenges that you have already overcome in your life by God's Grace. How has Jesus shown Himself faithful and strong in your life? Those victories can also become words of your testimony (about Jesus).

"Praise Yahweh, my soul, and don't forget all his benefits; who forgives all your sins; who heals all your diseases; who redeems your life from destruction; who crowns you with loving kindness and tender mercies; who satisfies your desire with good things, so that your youth is renewed like the eagle's." (Psalms 103:2-5 WEB)

When you remember all His benefits, it will empower and energize the word of your testimony to defeat a new giant that you are facing.

David declared that God who delivered him out of the paw of the lion and out of the paw of the bear will also deliver him out of the hand of Goliath.

"who delivered us out of so great a death, and does deliver; on whom we have set our hope that he will also still deliver us;" (2 Corinthians 1:10 WEB)

Likewise, you can boast in the Lord about the times that Jesus has delivered you from past challenges, how He is working on delivering you now, and that He will continue to deliver you from all enemies in the future!

Chapter 14: Lavish Angelic Protection Against your Demonic Enemies

"One of his servants said, "No, my lord, O king; but Elisha, the prophet who is in Israel, tells the king of Israel the words that you speak in your bedroom." He said, "Go and see where he is, that I may send and get him." He was told, "Behold, he is in Dothan." Therefore he sent horses, chariots, and a great army there. They came by night, and surrounded the city. When the servant of the man of God had risen early, and gone out, behold, an army with horses and chariots was around the city. His servant said to him, "Alas, my master! What shall we do?" He answered, "Don't be afraid; for those who are with us are more than those who are with them." Elisha prayed, and said, "Yahweh, please open his eyes, that he may see." Yahweh opened the young man's eyes; and he saw: and behold, the mountain was full of horses and chariots of fire around Elisha. When they came down to him, Elisha prayed to Yahweh, and said, "Please strike this people with

blindness." He struck them with blindness according to Elisha's word." (2 Kings 6:12-18 WEB)

When the king of Syria wanted to capture Elisha for spilling war secrets, he sent a great army to do it.

The Syrian army of mortal men and horses surrounded the city of Dothan.

But Elisha was not afraid because he knew that the powerful angelic armies protecting him far outnumbered the enemies who came against him.

When we see opposition in the natural (often triggered by demonic forces), we can remain at peace because God's angels are stationed all around you, to keep you in all your ways.

You may be thinking, "But I'm not Elisha the prophet. He is important and precious to God, but I'm not even serving God at church."

""For I tell you, among those who are born of women there is not a greater prophet than John the Baptizer, yet he who is least in God's Kingdom is greater than he."" (Luke 7:28 WEB)

Jesus said that John the Baptist was the greatest prophet at the time, even greater than Elisha, but even the least born-again believer in God's kingdom is greater than John.

This means that you are greater than Elisha and also far more precious. You are a new creation in Christ, a royal priest, thoroughly cleansed by the blood of Jesus. It is no surprise that powerful angelic armies will be guarding you in all your ways.

Aside from waging spiritual warfare by using spiritual weapons like the blood of Jesus and the word of your testimony, you have God's angels to assist you, even when you are not actively waging war.

"For he will put his angels in charge of you, to guard you in all your ways. They will bear you up in their hands, so that you won't dash your foot against a stone. You will tread on the lion and cobra. You will trample the young lion and the serpent underfoot." (Psalms 91:11-13 WEB)

Meditate on this: every believer has angels (plural and not singular) guarding them in all their ways. That is lavish protection, like a little child having six highly trained bodyguards for protection.

Why does God assign so much protection for you? There are two reasons: it is a dangerous world with many demons who target believers for attacks, and also because God loves you so much that He wants all your needs to be promptly and attentively met.

Each day, I like to pray with my family, declaring that God's angels are guarding us in all our ways. It is important to actively receive the promises of God, to give consent for God to protect my loved ones, my possessions and myself.

Only God knows how many times we have been rescued from Satan's dangerous traps thanks to angelic intervention. When you are protected by angels, no ambush can succeed against you, and you are free to trample the young lion and the serpent (pictures of Satan and his demons) underfoot by taking authority over them in the name of Jesus.

When the apostle Paul was arrested as a prisoner, forty Jews who were zealous for the Law of Moses secretly swore an oath to assassinate him. However, by God's intervention, this scheme was revealed to the Roman commanding officer, who then deployed four hundred and seventy soldiers in total to escort Paul to Felix the governor.

"He called to himself two of the centurions, and said, "Prepare two hundred soldiers to go as far as Caesarea, with seventy horsemen, and two hundred men armed with spears, at the third hour of the night." He asked them to provide animals, that they might set Paul on one, and bring him safely to Felix the governor." (Acts 23:23-24 WEB)

Four hundred and seventy soldiers to protect one Christian? Can you see this picture of lavish protection? The number of escorting soldiers was more than ten times the number of Paul's enemies. There are more who are with you than those who are against you.

When I received this revelation from the Holy Spirit, He then brought me to Psalm 27:2, corresponding to the first digit of the number of each individual type of soldiers deployed for Paul's sake. Take a look:

"When evildoers came at me to eat up my flesh, even my adversaries and my foes, they stumbled and fell." (Psalms 27:2 WEB)

"Evildoers", "adversaries" and "foes"—three types of enemies. In response, God has already prepared "soldiers", "horsemen" and "spearmen" to make them utterly stumble and fall—Hallelujah!

Chapter 15: It is Dangerous to Intentionally Harm God's People

"When Jehu had come to Jezreel, Jezebel heard of it; and she painted her eyes, and adorned her head, and looked out at the window. As Jehu entered in at the gate, she said, "Do you come in peace, Zimri, you murderer of your master?" He lifted up his face to the window, and said, "Who is on my side? Who?" Two or three eunuchs looked out at him. He said, "Throw her down!" So they threw her down; and some of her blood was sprinkled on the wall, and on the horses. Then he trampled her under foot. When he had come in, he ate and drank. Then he said, "See now to this cursed woman, and bury her; for she is a king's daughter." They went to bury her, but they found no more of her than the skull, the feet, and the palms of her hands. Therefore they came back, and told him. He said, "This is Yahweh's word, which he spoke by his servant Elijah the Tishbite, saying, 'The dogs will eat the flesh of Jezebel on the plot of Jezreel, and the body of

Jezebel will be as dung on the face of the field on Jezreel's land, so that they won't say, "This is Jezebel."'" (2 Kings 9:30-37 WEB)

Sometimes we see evil triumphing in the world and wonder if God really judges the wicked and protects His people.

The Lord led me to this judgment which He executed upon Jezebel. She was the pagan queen who was married to Ahab. She worshipped Baal and led Israel into idolatry and sexual immorality.

It is foolish to try and harm God's people. The nation of Israel is God's covenant people, and so are we, the church of Jesus Christ.

When unbelievers try to harm believers, they are putting themselves in a very dangerous position, because God may kill them if He deems it necessary.

Look at Jezebel's end. She was born as a king's daughter who grew up to become a vain woman who had riches, power, and the privilege to beautify herself. But she died in a most gruesome way, being totally disfigured by the fall, and being trampled on. Her corpse was then eaten by dogs until only her skull, feet and palms were left.

Does God pour out judgment upon the world today for their sins? In general, no. But those who deliberately persecute the church, or the nation of Israel will be destroyed if they do not repent.

Some examples of this happening in New Testament times which I will not elaborate on are Ananias and Sapphira who tried to infiltrate the early church and destroy it from within, and king Herod who killed the apostle James. These unbelievers purposely set out to harm the church but were killed by God before they could continue any further. You can read about them in the Book of Acts.

Ananias and Sapphira tried to harm the church subtly, whereas king Herod did so blatantly. Whether your enemy comes hidden in disguise or openly and arrogantly, God will deal severely with them.

"Bless those who persecute you; bless, and don't curse...Don't seek revenge yourselves, beloved, but give place to God's wrath. For it is written, "Vengeance belongs to me; I will repay, says the Lord."" (Romans 12:14, 19 WEB)

Perhaps that is why the apostle Paul taught believers to bless those who persecuted them and not to curse their persecutors—if not their persecutors would surely come to a horrible end.

It is perfectly fine to hope for the persecution to come to a swift end, but our hearts should beat like God's, desiring that all be saved through faith in Jesus, not wishing that any should perish in their sins.

To the church of Thyatira, Jesus had a message for them which mentioned the name "Jezebel".

"But I have this against you, that you tolerate your woman, Jezebel, who calls herself a prophetess. She teaches and seduces my servants to commit sexual immorality, and to eat things sacrificed to idols. I gave her time to repent, but she refuses to repent of her sexual immorality. Behold, I will throw her into a bed, and those who commit adultery with her into great oppression, unless they repent of her works. I will kill her children with Death, and all the assemblies will know that I am he who searches the minds and hearts. I will give to each one of you according to your deeds. But to you I say, to the rest who are in Thyatira, as many as don't have this teaching, who don't know what some call 'the deep things of Satan,' to you I say, I am not putting any other burden on you." (Revelation 2:20-24 WEB)

There was a false prophetess in the Thyatira assembly who was teaching the church to commit sexual immorality and idolatry.

Whether her name was literally Jezebel, we do not know, but Jesus probably used that name to draw the similarity between her and queen Jezebel: they were both women who led God's people into the sins of sexual immorality and idolatry.

Notice that Jesus first gives the perpetrator time to repent, but if they do not cease from harming His church, He will have to stop them Himself to protect the church.

Jesus killed that false prophetess by allowing Death to throw her into a bed (of sickness)—she fell gravely sick and died. Her unrepentant followers also met the same fate.

Do not be afraid if Satan sends persecution your way. Besides your usage of spiritual weapons and the angels guarding you in all your ways, Jesus Himself protects you from anyone who dares to intentionally harm you. He will kill them if necessary.

You are safe in God's mighty hands, so live with bold confidence in His love!

Chapter 16: Purify your Faith for Breakthroughs by Hearing the Gospel

"Yahweh said to Joshua, "Behold, I have given Jericho into your hand, with its king and the mighty men of valor. All of your men of war shall march around the city, going around the city once. You shall do this six days. Seven priests shall bear seven trumpets of rams' horns before the ark. On the seventh day, you shall march around the city seven times, and the priests shall blow the trumpets. It shall be that when they make a long blast with the ram's horn, and when you hear the sound of the trumpet, all the people shall shout with a great shout; and the city wall shall fall down flat, and the people shall go up, every man straight in front of him."" (Joshua 6:2-5 WEB)

When Joshua and the children of Israel marched around the city of Jericho, they were physically walking in a circle, yet in their hearts, they were actually ascending higher—ever closer to their victory.

Joshua told them to be silent—to restrain their fleshly complaints and murmurings. Instead, they were to listen to the trumpets of ram's horns being sounded.

Since they could not talk or do anything else, the trumpet sound possibly reminded them that a ram had to be slain to make that trumpet.

Some probably recalled how Yahweh provided a ram in Isaac's place for Abraham. Who does this ram represent? It is a picture of our Lord Jesus Christ who was slain as the perfect atoning sacrifice for our sins.

In other words, every time the priests sounded the trumpets of ram's horns, they were unconsciously proclaiming the Lord's death at the cross.

When you face difficulties in certain areas of your life, they could be manifestations of a Satanic stronghold that is in your mind—like a heavily fortified city of Jericho.

The walls of Jericho were extremely thick. Carnal weapons could not break through. Likewise, as we have already learned, we need to use powerful spiritual weapons which far exceed carnal weapons. The Gospel of Jesus Christ is one such weapon, packed full of the dunamis (miracle-working power) of God.

The walls of Jericho did not crack at all during the first six days. Even though it seems like there is nothing happening in the natural, every time you hear the Gospel of Jesus Christ and believe it, your ascending higher in your heart, closer to the state of pure faith. Time invested into hearing the Gospel is never wasted time.

It may not take a literal seven days, but the number "seven" represents perfection or completion. In other words, when unbelief has been perfectly cast out of your heart through receiving the Gospel (good news) of God's love, grace, and mercy towards you, then the Jericho in your mind is ready to fall.

When you confess and believe in your victory based on Jesus' finished work at the cross, those wrong beliefs which are holding you captive shall surely crumble.

It is easy to shout at any time, but the journey to an effective, wall-destroying shout is all about casting unbelief out of your heart. There is no power in shouting with your mouth while your heart still does not believe what you are saying.

It may seem really repetitive, but the role that God assigned for us as believers is simple: just keep hearing the good news about Jesus, believe it and speak forth what you believe. That is the kind of faith that demolishes the walls of Jericho.

God revealed to Joshua the appointed time of seven days before the walls would fall, for the children of Israel to capture and plunder the city. However, most of the time, God does not tell you exactly when the strongholds in your mind will fall.

Instead of asking how long, just make a habit of receiving the preached Gospel daily. Pure faith will eventually arise to destroy the thick walls of wrong beliefs obstructing your inheritance in Christ. The stronghold will fall, and your demonic enemies will have to flee from you when the time comes!

Chapter 17: The Anointing Oil Breaks Satanic Yokes

"It will happen in that day, that his burden will depart from off your shoulder, and his yoke from off your neck, and the yoke shall be destroyed because of the anointing oil." (Isaiah 10:27 WEB)

A natural yoke is a device fastened over two animals' necks, attaching them together. Similarly, a Satanic yoke is a connection that attaches you to a demon, which subjects you to oppression.

Just as a yoked animal is forced to move when the other animal moves, the demon can influence your soul and body to a limited extent.

Satanic yokes can be formed when you engage in activities like occult practices, worshiping idols, or even through sexual immorality when you have intercourse with a person that has demons attached to him or her. During sex, you and the other person become one flesh. This gives access to the demons.

Just as the demonic can be transferred, the power of the Holy Spirit can also be transferred.

"God worked special miracles by the hands of Paul, so that even handkerchiefs or aprons were carried away from his body to the sick, and the diseases departed from them, and the evil spirits went out." (Acts 19:11-12 WEB)

Did you know that the power of the Holy Spirit (the anointing) can be transferred and stored in objects?

When people placed handkerchiefs and aprons on the apostle Paul and put them on the sick, diseases departed, and demons were cast out.

The anointing oil is a powerful spiritual weapon that destroys Satanic yokes. It is a picture of the Holy Spirit who is depicted as oil in the Bible.

Olive oil is produced by crushing olives in an olive press. This is a picture of how Jesus was crushed starting from the Garden of Gethsemane (which means "oil press") all the way to the cross. Jesus was crushed so that the Holy Spirit could be poured out upon the church, starting from the Day of Pentecost.

Therefore, when you apply the anointing oil, you are proclaiming Jesus' finished work at the cross and the power of the Holy Spirit that you have access to now because of that atoning sacrifice.

It is not a must to use olive oil, even though it is the clearest type of what Jesus did for us.

"It shall not be poured on man's flesh, and do not make any like it, according to its composition. It is holy. It shall be holy to you. Whoever compounds any like it, or whoever puts any of it on a stranger, he shall be cut off from his people.""" (Exodus 30:32-33 WEB)

Under the Old Covenant of the Law, God told Moses to make a holy anointing oil and that no one should make another like it according to its composition. Elsewhere in the Bible, whenever the anointing oil is mentioned, it does not say that you must use a specific type of oil.

This is in line with God's ways. His ways are inclusive and easy to follow, whether you are rich or poor, and no matter where you live in the world.

You do not have to climb Mount Everest to find a special flower that produces the only oil you can use to make anointing oil. On the other hand, the devil's ways are exclusive and secretive, whereby only certain selected elite members of his organizations have access to the 'deep things of Satan'.

Feel free to use any kind of oil to make anointing oil. I prefer olive oil because it is a clear symbol of the Holy Spirit, so I use that.

By praying over a bottle of oil, you can transfer the power of the Holy Spirit to it and make it a holy anointing oil. The word holy in Hebrew, "kadosh", means to be specially set apart. When you pray over a bottle of oil, you are doing that.

You can use your own words, but this is an example: "Dear Abba God, I declare that this bottle of oil is set apart as a holy anointing oil, so that whoever is anointed with this oil will be healed from sicknesses and be delivered from demons. The power of the Holy Spirit rests upon this oil to break bondages and set the captives free. In Jesus' name I pray, Amen."

Even in the New Testament, we are taught to apply the anointing oil upon the sick and pray over them for healing.

"Is any among you sick? Let him call for the elders of the assembly, and let them pray over him, anointing him with oil in the name of the Lord, and the prayer of faith will heal him who is sick, and the Lord will raise him up. If he has committed sins, he will be forgiven." (James 5:14-15 WEB)

Notice that it does not say it has to be a specific type of oil. Any oil is fine because it is just symbolic of the Holy Spirit's power.

Do not question why it has to be oil and not sand or something else. It is beneficial to follow God's ways because He has sanctioned it.

When you use the anointing oil, God's power to break Satanic yokes is released. The sick will be healed and the demonically oppressed will be delivered.

If Satan has bound you in any way, apply the anointing oil over the affected thing and the prayer of faith will release God's dunamis (miracle-working power) for your situation!

Chapter 18: Your God is Stronger than the Giants

"Yahweh spoke to Moses, saying, "Send men, that they may spy out the land of Canaan, which I give to the children of Israel. Of every tribe of their fathers, you shall send a man, every one a prince among them." (Numbers 13:1-2 WEB)

Yahweh instructed the children of Israel to spy out the land of Canaan which He had promised to them.

One prince from each tribe was sent out, and the twelve spies surveyed the land for forty days and brought back a report of the land.

"They went and came to Moses, to Aaron, and to all the congregation of the children of Israel, to the wilderness of Paran, to Kadesh; and brought back word to them and to all the congregation. They showed them the fruit of the land. They told him, and said, "We came to the land where you sent

us. Surely it flows with milk and honey, and this is its fruit. However the people who dwell in the land are strong, and the cities are fortified and very large. Moreover, we saw the children of Anak there. Amalek dwells in the land of the South. The Hittite, the Jebusite, and the Amorite dwell in the hill country. The Canaanite dwells by the sea, and along the side of the Jordan." Caleb stilled the people before Moses, and said, "Let us go up at once, and possess it; for we are well able to overcome it!" But the men who went up with him said, "We aren't able to go up against the people; for they are stronger than we." They brought up an evil report of the land which they had spied out to the children of Israel, saying, "The land, through which we have gone to spy it out, is a land that eats up its inhabitants; and all the people who we saw in it are men of great stature. There we saw the Nephilim, the sons of Anak, who come from the Nephilim. We were in our own sight as grasshoppers, and so we were in their sight.""* (Numbers 13:26-33 WEB)*

The princes of the tribes who spied out the land can be a picture of leaders in the church.

Some so-called leaders are like the ten spies who brought back an evil report of the land. They read the Bible and interpret God as angry and unwilling to help believers. Then, they magnify the power of Satan, causing believers to be afraid of punishment from God and fear Satan's power.

Such leaders are not saying that the land is not good. They say that God's blessings of prosperity, health, healing, peace, and fruitfulness are all good, but it is difficult to receive because the demonic enemies are too strong. They make the giants seem to be stronger than God.

For example, a preacher may say that sometimes God heals, but sometimes He does not. So, you will never know if it is His will to heal you or not.

God calls all these "evil" reports because they are not true. God had promised the land of Canaan to the children of Israel, and that rhema (What God is currently saying) carried the authority and empowerment to accomplish the task, if they had faith in it.

What kind of Christian leaders are you listening to? Are you hearing messages that ask you to be careful of Satan who is extremely powerful, that God does not heal people today, that He does not give financial prosperity, that He is angry with you when you fall into sin and only accepts you when you do not sin?

When you believe these kinds of messages, you are still saved and will go to Heaven, but you will not get to enjoy the manifestation of God's gracious promises in this mortal lifetime.

"Joshua the son of Nun and Caleb the son of Jephunneh, who were of those who spied out the land, tore their clothes. They spoke to all the congregation of the children of Israel, saying, "The land, which we passed through to spy it out, is an exceeding good land. If Yahweh delights in us, then he will bring us into this land, and give it to us; a land which flows with milk and honey. Only don't rebel against Yahweh, neither fear the people of the land;

for they are bread for us. Their defense is removed from over them, and Yahweh is with us. Don't fear them."" (Numbers 14:6-9 WEB)

Instead of listening to messages that are essentially the voice of the serpent, listen to leaders who have miracle-receiving faith like Joshua and Caleb.

The other ten spies also agreed that it was an exceedingly good land, but the difference is that Joshua and Caleb believed that God was for them to give them the land. The two men confessed that the giants were weak, like defenceless bread to be eaten because God was giving favor to the children of Israel.

"surely they shall not see the land which I swore to their fathers, neither shall any of those who despised me see it. But my servant Caleb, because he had another spirit with him, and has followed me fully, him I will bring into the land into which he went. His offspring shall possess it...Tell them, 'As I live, says Yahweh, surely as you have spoken in my ears, so will I do to you. Your dead bodies shall fall in this wilderness; and all who were counted of you, according to your whole number, from twenty years old and upward, who have murmured against me, surely you shall not come into the land, concerning which I swore that I would make you dwell therein, except Caleb the son of Jephunneh, and Joshua the son of Nun." (Numbers 14:23-24, 28-30 WEB)

What if God leads you in a path that has giants standing in the way? A giant can represent a seemingly insurmountable problem that you are facing.

God said that Caleb had another spirit causing him to follow Him fully. Joshua and Caleb had a spirit of faith while the other ten spies had a spirit of unbelief.

God's plan for Israel was to bring them out of Egypt, then through the Red Sea, and into the land of Canaan by going through the wilderness and the river Jordan. Most of the children of Israel only followed God halfway. They went into the wilderness and were doomed to die there because they were afraid of the giants in the land of Canaan.

To follow God fully means that if He leads you in a path that has giants on it, you continue to walk down the path, confident that God will supply the grace to defeat those giants.

The giants are not there to destroy you, but to be like bread served on a plate, strengthening you. They are opportunities to exercise your faith in real-life situations.

Your job is not to know how to defeat the giants, but just to have faith that God will make a way to defeat them for you.

What words are you speaking into God's ears? Are they confessions of faith demonstrating a good opinion of Him, or are you declaring evil reports, saying that the giants will surely consume you? You will have what you say.

While the ten spies were thinking that the inhabitants of Canaan saw the children of Israel as weak grasshoppers, this is what the Canaanites were really thinking:

"She said to the men, "I know that Yahweh has given you the land, and that the fear of you has fallen upon us, and that all the inhabitants of the land melt away before you. For we have heard how Yahweh dried up the water of the Red Sea before you, when you came out of Egypt; and what you did to the two kings of the Amorites, who were beyond the Jordan, to Sihon and to Og, whom you utterly destroyed. As soon as we had heard it, our hearts melted, and there wasn't any more spirit in any man, because of you: for Yahweh your God, he is God in heaven above, and on earth beneath." (Joshua 2:9-11 WEB)

The Canaanites, even the towering giants, were shivering in fear. They were not afraid because of the children of Israel, but they were afraid because Yahweh God was fighting for Israel!

The hearts of Israel's enemies had melted away. If the children of Israel had obeyed God and attacked, they would have surely possessed the land without having to wander forty years in the wilderness.

"You believe that God is one. You do well. The demons also believe, and shudder." (James 2:19 WEB)

Likewise, Satan and his demons are actually afraid when they try to attack you. Not because they fear you, but they fear the God who lives inside you and who has supplied you with powerful spiritual weapons and lavish angelic protection.

That is why they try so hard to deceive, distract and intimidate you. While you are still afraid of demons and fearful of God's judgment, you will remain defeated.

However, once you learn the way of faith and apply it, you will become an unstoppable conqueror through Christ Jesus!

Chapter 19: The Sting of Death is Gone

"Behold, I give you authority to tread on serpents and scorpions, and over all the power of the enemy. Nothing will in any way hurt you." (Luke 10:19 WEB)

Many troubles we experience in life are the work of Satan and his demons, represented by the serpents and scorpions in the verse above. When they attack, do you know what to do?

The power of a serpent is in its poisonous bite, and the power of a scorpion is in its toxic sting. The serpent's mouth is in front, the scorpion's stinger is at the back.

Jesus is saying that He has given you authority and protection against the front, back and everything in-between of the enemy.

When you understand how to tread on your demonic enemies, you become immune to harm.

"'Death, where is your sting? Hades, where is your victory?" The sting of death is sin, and the power of sin is the law." (1 Corinthians 15:55-56 WEB)

Sin is the scorpion's poisonous sting which produces death. Satan wants people to nurture their sins so that their sowing into the flesh brings forth the mature fruit of death.

Sin produces death because of the Law (the Ten Commandments). A transgression of God's law brings the penalty of death and the curse of the Law. Without the Law, sin would not result in death.

For a born-again believer, sin has become powerless to kill him (the spirit) because the believer has shared in Jesus' death and has passed from death into life. He has been irreversibly saved.

"'Most certainly I tell you, he who hears my word, and believes him who sent me, has eternal life, and doesn't come into judgment, but has passed out of death into life." (John 5:24 WEB)

Sin is also unable to bring the curse upon a believer because Jesus has redeemed us from the curse of the Law, having become a curse Himself at the cross.

"Christ redeemed us from the curse of the law, having become a curse for us. For it is written, "Cursed is everyone who hangs on a tree," that the blessing

of Abraham might come on the Gentiles through Christ Jesus; that we might receive the promise of the Spirit through faith." (Galatians 3:13-14 WEB)

However, many believers do not know these. When up against a believer, Satan is like a scorpion without a sting. He still tries to deceive believers that they can lose their salvation and that God curses them when they sin. Making a Christian think that God is against him destroys his faith because who can resist the power of God?

Actually, the only way the sting can grow back is if you put yourself under the Law again. The moment you attempt works-based justification, it is like Satan's sting regenerates and is driven deep into your body, inflicting death through the curse of the Law.

"For as many as are of the works of the law are under a curse. For it is written, "Cursed is everyone who doesn't continue in all things that are written in the book of the law, to do them."" (Galatians 3:10 WEB)

Satan may come with lies like a serpent and say, "You sinned again. You are hopeless. God's curse is upon you. God is going to destroy you because you keep repeating your sins and are unrepentant."

He heaps accusations and condemnation upon you. The moment you believe him, you are stung by the scorpion. The curse of the Law takes effect in your life because you have effectively put yourself under the covenant of the Law as a transgressor.

Based on the principle of sowing and reaping, sin still bears the fruit of death, causing sickness, depression, infirmity, aging, and finally the death of the body, but sin cannot cause you to lose your salvation or bring you under God's curse.

God is for you, not against you. His favor continually shines upon you and it is not by your performance, but by the grace of God, made possible through Jesus' finished work at the cross.

When you fall because of sin, it is by the grace of God that you can immediately pick yourself up again. Do not cut yourself off from that supply by being self-condemned.

In your war against Satan's temptations, sometimes you will fall—and God knows that. But you can dust yourself off and get up again by receiving the grace and mercy of God. Do not allow Satan to trick you into thinking that God's curse is upon you.

The scorpion's sting has been removed and the Law does not apply to you, so let it stay that way. You are a child of God under the New Covenant of Grace who is led by the Holy Spirit!

Chapter 20: The Value of the Blood of Jesus

"For the life of the flesh is in the blood; and I have given it to you on the altar to make atonement for your souls: for it is the blood that makes atonement by reason of the life." (Leviticus 17:11 WEB)

The Law says an eye for an eye, a tooth for a tooth. A life for a life. The wages of sin is death.

The shedding of blood makes payment for sin because the life of a being is contained in its blood.

Have you ever wondered why Satanic rituals are often depicted to require a sacrifice of blood and even semen? Demons do not have the power to create something out of nothing.

Magic takes from an existing source to transform it for a different purpose.

They can use the life force (in Hebrew it is called "chayil") that is in fresh blood and semen as a source of power to alter something in the natural world.

"Then Pharaoh also called for the wise men and the sorcerers. They also, the magicians of Egypt, did the same thing with their enchantments. For they each cast down their rods, and they became serpents: but Aaron's rod swallowed up their rods...Moses and Aaron did so, as Yahweh commanded; and he lifted up the rod, and struck the waters that were in the river, in the sight of Pharaoh, and in the sight of his servants; and all the waters that were in the river were turned to blood. The fish that were in the river died; and the river became foul, and the Egyptians couldn't drink water from the river; and the blood was throughout all the land of Egypt. The magicians of Egypt did the same thing with their enchantments; and Pharaoh's heart was hardened, and he didn't listen to them; as Yahweh had spoken." (Exodus 7:11-12, 20-22 WEB)

The magicians of Pharaoh were able to transform their wooden rods into the likeness of serpents and they could also turn water into the likeness of blood. These are real magical acts, but they had to offer a sacrifice to cast those spells—probably a blood sacrifice.

After that, they also used magic to bring up huge swarms of frogs into Egypt just like Moses and Aaron did. However, for the fourth plague, the magicians were unable to replicate it.

"Yahweh said to Moses, "Tell Aaron, 'Stretch out your rod, and strike the dust of the earth, that it may become lice throughout all the land of Egypt.'" They did so; and Aaron stretched out his hand with his rod, and struck the dust of the earth, and there were lice on man, and on animal; all the dust of the earth became lice throughout all the land of Egypt. The magicians tried with their enchantments to produce lice, but they couldn't. There were lice on man, and on animal. Then the magicians said to Pharaoh, "This is God's finger:" and Pharaoh's heart was hardened, and he didn't listen to them; as Yahweh had spoken." (Exodus 8:16-19 WEB)

In the magicians' first magical act, notice that the rods were still called "rods" after they were transformed into serpents. This means that they did not become real animals, but just took on the appearance and likeness of serpents.

However, to turn dust into lice means to be creating life. It is like how God formed the body of Adam from the dust of the ground and breathed life into him. The magicians had no power to do that.

Demonic magic is limited—it cannot create something out of nothing, and it cannot create life.

The more valuable the creature, the more valuable its blood is. The blood of animals is inferior to the blood of humans.

"For if the blood of goats and bulls, and the ashes of a heifer sprinkling those who have been defiled, sanctify to the cleanness of the flesh: how much more will the blood of Christ, who through the eternal Spirit offered himself without defect to God, cleanse your conscience from dead works to serve the living God? For this reason he is the mediator of a new covenant, since a death has occurred for the redemption of the transgressions that were under the first covenant, that those who have been called may receive the promise of the eternal inheritance." (Hebrews 9:13-15 WEB)

Under the Law, spilling the blood of unblemished bulls and goats as offerings to God are sufficient to sanctify and cleanse the flesh (the body and soul) but not the spirit.

Even if a human's life were to be offered on your behalf, it would not be able to pay for your sins because there is sin in his or her blood, making it an unacceptable sacrifice.

Now consider the blood of Christ. Jesus is the Son of God, and He is God.

The life of God offered as a payment for your sins. Now could that pay for your sins and cleanse you in body, soul, and spirit? Yes! It can even cleanse the whole creation of mankind because the value of God's life is infinitely more than the price of the world's sins.

The word "redemption" in the passage on the previous page is "apolutrosis" which means "a release effected by payment of a ransom."

The blood that Jesus spilled for you was a payment for your sin debt. The righteous requirements of the first covenant (the Law) has been paid in full, and you do not owe anything to God. You are not a debtor. In fact, there is a lot of balance credit and you have been adopted as God's son.

Do you want to know how forgiven, holy, pure, blameless, and righteous you are? Look at the cross and the blood that Jesus shed for you.

When you pray, "By the blood of Jesus," you're saying that your request is not based on your obedience (which is the Old Covenant of the Law) but based on Jesus' perfect obedience at the cross.

No wonder the blood of Jesus is a weapon to overcome Satan. No matter how many fiery darts of lies he shoots at you, as long as you know the value of the blood of Jesus, nothing can make you doubt how forgiven and righteous you are, and no one can make you feel disqualified.

You stand permanently in God's favor because Jesus exceedingly overpaid your sin debt!

Chapter 21: God's Love, Not your Love

"One of them, a lawyer, asked him a question, testing him. "Teacher, which is the greatest commandment in the law?" Jesus said to him, "'You shall love the Lord your God with all your heart, with all your soul, and with all your mind.' This is the first and great commandment." (Matthew 22:35-38 WEB)

The passage above has become a stumbling block to many believers who do not understand the context of Jesus' words.

Jesus was simply replying the lawyer's question about what the greatest commandment in the Law is. He was not saying that we need to love God like that in order to be saved or accepted by God.

To the legalistic ones like the Pharisees and scribes, Jesus gave the full measure of the Law to bring them to the end of themselves, so that they would stop boasting in their own righteousness. On the other hand, to sinners who freely admitted their sinfulness and need for Him, He extended kindness and grace.

The irony is that once you start trying to love God, you fall into works-based justification and self-condemnation whenever you slip up. Instead of loving God, you will end up feeling defeated under the curse of the Law.

Satan comes to you, sowing seeds of condemnation, saying that you do not love God enough. He points to your failures and says that they are evidence that you do not love God.

Then, he even makes you compare yourself with others, saying that others love God more than you, and that you are not worthy to be called a Christian.

All these tactics are attempts to bring you under works-based justification, so that the curse of the Law will be activated in your life.

As long as you are still focused on what you have to do to love God or to get Him to love you, you will find yourself slipping further and further from your desired goal.

"Whoever is born of God doesn't commit sin, because his seed remains in him; and he can't sin, because he is born of God." (1 John 3:9 WEB)

All born-again believers have the seed of God in their spirits—like a spiritual DNA. They have the deep desire in their spirits to do what is pleasing to God and will not agree with the flesh to stay in a sinful lifestyle. The key is to learn how to receive the power to love God and effortlessly do what is pleasing to God.

Just focus on God's perfect love for you. He proved His love by sending Jesus to die on the cross for your sins. Would you let your only beloved son die for your wicked enemies who hate you? You would not, but God the Father did it so that we could be saved and not perish in our sins.

"By this God's love was revealed in us, that God has sent his one and only Son into the world that we might live through him. In this is love, not that we loved God, but that he loved us, and sent his Son as the atoning sacrifice for our sins." (1 John 4:9-10 WEB)

Our love for God is not even deserving to be called love. It fluctuates and is unreliable.

"One who has my commandments, and keeps them, that person is one who loves me. One who loves me will be loved by my Father, and I will love him, and will reveal myself to him."" (John 14:21 WEB)

Love towards God is proven by keeping His commandments under Grace—to believe in Jesus Christ and to love one another just as Jesus has loved us.

Our daily actions often fall short of God's glory. We sometimes have unbelief and do what is unloving towards our fellow men.

If it is up to your love for God to maintain your salvation, then it is no different from the Law.

We must understand that love for God and fellow men flows as a fruit of being well-nourished in God's love. You cannot give love when you are empty—you must first receive it abundantly from God.

If you want to love God, allow God's love to do its perfect work in your heart.

It will transform you from the inside out if you just meditate on His love and receive it afresh through the Scriptures.

As you pray in tongues, the rivers of living water in you will also wash you with God's love like a warm bath.

It just takes a renewal of your mind. Simply focus on God's love for you, not on your love for God. That is how to bear good fruits of love!

Chapter 22: Actively Remain in your Safe Fortress

"So she caught him, and kissed him. With an impudent face she said to him: "Sacrifices of peace offerings are with me. Today I have paid my vows. Therefore I came out to meet you, to diligently seek your face, and I have found you. I have spread my couch with carpets of tapestry, with striped cloths of the yarn of Egypt. I have perfumed my bed with myrrh, aloes, and cinnamon. Come, let's take our fill of loving until the morning. Let's solace ourselves with loving. For my husband isn't at home. He has gone on a long journey. He has taken a bag of money with him. He will come home at the full moon." With persuasive words, she led him astray. With the flattering of her lips, she seduced him. He followed her immediately, as an ox goes to the slaughter, as a fool stepping into a noose. Until an arrow strikes through his liver, as a bird hurries to the snare, and doesn't know that it will cost his life." (Proverbs 7:13-23 WEB)

Seduction is one of Satan's temptation tactics. He presents an act of sin as a delectable, attractive treat.

Just as the prostitute in the passage deceived the young man saying that her husband will never find out, Satan also tries to trick you into believing that there will be no consequences to your sin.

It is true that there is no condemnation for those who are in Christ Jesus (Romans 8:1). God does not condemn you because He already sent Jesus to pay for your sins at the cross.

Even though God is not punishing you for your sins, and you cannot lose your salvation, sowing to the flesh still bears fruit to death. These are earthly consequences reaped based on the principle of sowing and reaping.

"So then, brothers, we are debtors, not to the flesh, to live after the flesh. For if you live after the flesh, you must die; but if by the Spirit you put to death the deeds of the body, you will live. For as many as are led by the Spirit of God, these are children of God." (Romans 8:12-14 WEB)

Notice that the apostle Paul is addressing believers in the passage above by saying "brothers, we". Living after the flesh means to indulge in habitual sin. If you sow seeds of sin, you will reap the fruit of death.

"But each one is tempted when he is drawn away by his own lust, and enticed. Then the lust, when it has conceived, bears sin; and the sin, when it is full grown, produces death." (James 1:14-15 WEB)

Death includes sickness, depression, or poverty, infirmity, and the fully ripened form of it is bodily death.

I have ever heard of a saying, "Everyone is allowed to have one vice". Those who think that nurturing a sinful habit has no consequences are fooling themselves.

Constantly watering a seed of sin will surely cause it to bear the mature fruit of death. Satan will use that one vice to bring in all sorts of death into your life.

"Now therefore, sons, listen to me. Pay attention to the words of my mouth. Don't let your heart turn to her ways. Don't go astray in her paths, for she has thrown down many wounded. Yes, all her slain are a mighty army. Her house is the way to Sheol, going down to the rooms of death." (Proverbs 7:24-27 WEB)

The young man's big mistake was to stand there and let the prostitute deliver her convincing sales pitch to him.

When Satan comes with a temptation, it is time to resist it by confessing God's word, and quickly fleeing from the situation where you are being tempted.

The prostitute slew a mighty army—those who think that they are strong in the flesh and can handle temptation through willpower and discipline. As we have studied, you cannot overcome Satan and his demons by using carnal weapons.

If you 'try your best' to say no to sin and to logically tell yourself why it is not worth it, you will end up persuading yourself to sin "just this once and that nothing bad will happen".

"After these things, his master's wife set her eyes on Joseph; and she said, "Lie with me." But he refused, and said to his master's wife, "Behold, my master doesn't know what is with me in the house, and he has put all that he has into my hand. No one is greater in this house than I am, and he has not kept back anything from me but you, because you are his wife. How then can I do this great wickedness, and sin against God?" As she spoke to Joseph day by day, he didn't listen to her, to lie by her, or to be with her. About this time, he went into the house to do his work, and there were none of the men of the house inside. She caught him by his garment, saying, "Lie with me!" He left his garment in her hand, and ran outside." (Genesis 39:7-12 WEB)

Potiphar's wife used the same tactic to tempt Joseph—she seduced him at a time when her husband was not at home.

However, Joseph was not foolish enough to think that no one would know or that there would be no consequences to sinning.

He was keenly aware that God was watching over him. His heart was full of gratitude and worship towards God.

Joseph did not trust in the strength of his flesh because he ran away when the temptation was strong. We must also learn to remove ourselves from sources of temptation.

Do not linger around to listen to the serpent's sales pitch. Eve did that and she ate from the tree of knowledge of good and evil.

When you remain at places of temptation, you are giving Satan a tactical advantage. However, when you are plugged in to God's word and consistently hearing it, you are the one with the tactical advantage.

It is like changing the battlefield, putting yourself at a high vantage point.

"I will say of Yahweh, "He is my refuge and my fortress; my God, in whom I trust.""" (Psalms 91:2 WEB)

Do you know the difference between a refuge and a fortress? A refuge is a place to flee to when you are ambushed by an unforeseen enemy attack.

On the other hand, a fortress is a heavily fortified place where you station yourself in when you already anticipate the enemy's attack. There are many good hiding spots in a fortress, allowing you to shoot at the enemy safely while making it extremely difficult for the enemy to aim at you.

When your place your faith in Jesus, it is like stationing yourself in the most secure fortress. Satan's lies, seductions and intimidations cannot even affect you. However, if you have neglected God's word for a while and are especially susceptible to temptations, you can still flee to Jesus as your refuge in crucial moments.

Do not be like the young man who was drawn out into the streets at night, like a person whose heart is filled with wonderment towards the things of the world. It is not safe to let your heart roam in the dark streets.

"Even as the Father has loved me, I also have loved you. Remain in my love." (John 15:9 WEB)

By receiving messages of Jesus' love for you every day, you can actively remain in your safe fortress.

When your heart is well-established in His love, the serpent's temptations cannot prosper against you!

Chapter 23: Praying with Authority, not Timidity

"He called to himself his twelve disciples, and gave them authority over unclean spirits, to cast them out, and to heal every disease and every sickness." (Matthew 10:1 WEB)

The word translated as "authority" in the verse above is "exousia" in the Greek. It has the meaning of "conferred power to act".

A person can attempt an action and fail because there is no power to succeed. However, when God gives you authority, it means He backs up your actions with His power.

With this authority, Jesus' twelve disciples cast out demons and healed people from every type of sickness and disease.

You may say, "But I'm not one of the twelve disciples. Wasn't this authority only given specifically to them?"

Yes, Jesus only spoke to them in that verse, but it allowed us to see what happens when God gives authority to His people. It empowers them to do exactly what He said they could do.

The following words of Jesus are directed at you:

"These signs will accompany those who believe: in my name they will cast out demons; they will speak with new languages; they will take up serpents; and if they drink any deadly thing, it will in no way hurt them; they will lay hands on the sick, and they will recover."" (Mark 16:17-18 WEB)

"Those who believe" includes you if you are a born-again believer. Jesus has given you the authority to cast out demons, to pray in tongues, to be protected from serpents and poison, and to lay hands on the sick to heal them.

These are all supernatural things to be done in His name, meaning that Jesus empowers us to act as His representatives here on earth.

He also spoke with certainty, saying "they will" which means it will surely happen. It is definitely God's will for people to be delivered from demons and for them to recover from every sickness and disease when believers pray for them.

When a believer knows and exercises this authority, Satan has no choice but to flee. Unfortunately, many believers still do not fully believe that they have been given the authority to cast out demons and heal the sick.

It is the unbelief that hinders them, and the unbelief stems from ignorance of what the Scriptures actually say.

Imagine that you are a landlord trying to evict a tenant who is illegally living on your premises without paying rent. You cannot make him leave easily if you are not certain that you have the right to demand his eviction.

The tenant will give all sorts of excuses and justifications so that he can stay. You have to be sure that if the tenant refuses to leave he will have to face severe penalties from the authorities.

Better still, if you can print out the page of the government's law regarding this issue, the tenant will have no chance to lie.

When the tenant sees your certainty and determination, he will have no choice but to pack up and go, for fear of the severe consequences of staying.

You have to understand that you are not just hoping that God will back up your requests if He is in the mood or feeling especially generous.

No, Jesus' words are your guarantee that God will back up His words with power when you exercise that authority.

This is another 'Eve and the serpent' kind of scenario again. Two different voices with opposing views.

The serpent will not outrightly deny that Jesus said these words. He will try to make you question whether it applies to you, or just for a special group of extra-holy believers who do not sin.

The serpent will try to make you feel disqualified based on the Ten Commandments, bringing you back under works-based justification.

Are you going to listen to the serpent who makes you doubt the surety of God's word, or will you trust God's commandment (His word is law) which says He has given "those who believe" dominion over demons and sicknesses?

When you pray, expect the demons to flee and expect the sickness to go, just as you are sure that the sun will rise when morning comes!

Chapter 24: Satan Has Been Stripped of the Power of Death

"You were dead through your trespasses and the uncircumcision of your flesh. He made you alive together with him, having forgiven us all our trespasses, wiping out the handwriting in ordinances which was against us; and he has taken it out of the way, nailing it to the cross; having stripped the principalities and the powers, he made a show of them openly, triumphing over them in it." (Colossians 2:13-15 WEB)

The picture that the apostle Paul paints for us is that of a conqueror on horseback parading an enemy king and his subjects as defeated captives through the streets.

The defeated enemy king represents Satan. His ultimate weapon was the "handwriting of ordinances which was against us". This refers to the Ten Commandments of the Law which were handwritten on two tablets of stone.

Based on the Ten Commandments, we were once counted as transgressors and under the sentence of death. We were under the curse of the Law because of our sins.

Anytime Satan wanted to cause death, he only needed to point to the Ten Commandments as the basis for man to reap God's curse. The Law is holy, righteous, and true, and it will not be lenient to a sinner.

"Since then the children have shared in flesh and blood, he also himself in the same way partook of the same, that through death he might bring to nothing him who had the power of death, that is, the devil, and might deliver all of them who through fear of death were all their lifetime subject to bondage." (Hebrews 2:14-15 WEB)

By using the Ten Commandments as a weapon, Satan wielded the power of death.

However, by offering Himself as an atoning sacrifice on the cross, Jesus' precious blood overpaid for the sins of the world and His death established the New Covenant of Grace, effectively nailing the Ten Commandments to the cross.

This means that Satan has no more legal basis to wield the Law as an instrument of death against a believer, for a believer has passed from death to life, unable to die again. He has been perfectly cleansed from all records of sin because they have been imputed to Jesus.

Satan once ruled over mankind and the whole earth in the same capacity as Adam did, but through the cross, Jesus righteously redeemed everything that Adam lost.

If Satan accuses a Christian based on the Ten Commandments today, his argument will not hold up in the heavenly courts.

The Ten Commandments do not apply to a Christian because he is not under the Old Covenant of the Law. He has been permanently discharged from it.

The only way Satan can gain the upper hand is if he successfully deceives a Christian to believe that the Ten Commandments is still applicable to him (the Christian) today.

As a subtle serpent, he will never say that you can only be saved through keeping the Law. That will be too obviously wrong, and it only works on a minority of Christians.

The half-truth version is that you are saved by faith in Jesus, but you must be guided by the Ten Commandments so that you can live righteously.

The moment you believe that and try to live by the Ten Commandments, you are putting yourself under the works of the Law and come under a curse.

"For as many as are of the works of the law are under a curse. For it is written, "Cursed is everyone who doesn't continue in all things that are written in the book of the law, to do them."" (Galatians 3:10 WEB)

The Law is the knowledge of sin. It tells you what a crime against God is, but it never empowers you to live a holy life.

All born-again believers want to live righteous lives, but in place of the cold, inanimate tablets of the Ten Commandments, we have a living person to teach and empower us to do it—the Holy Spirit who resides in us.

Following the Holy Spirit is the highest form of obedience—to do so is to be led by God Himself.

"For as many as are led by the Spirit of God, these are children of God." (Romans 8:14 WEB)

The Law is for servants, but Grace is for the royal sons of God.

Instead of the fear of punishment, your motivation for obedience changes to "a response to God's abundant love for you".

Therefore, leave the Ten Commandments nailed to the cross, like the two tablets of stone hidden inside the Ark of the Covenant.

If you were to travel back in time to Solomon's temple in the Old Testament times, on the Day of Atonement, what you would see is the mercy seat on top of the Ark of the Covenant, with the blood of a sacrificial animal sprinkled on it.

It was the blood that atoned for the sins of Israel, sanctifying them to the cleanness of their flesh.

Likewise, when God looks at you today, He sees Jesus' blood that has been shed for the atonement of your sins.

Do not let the serpent trick you into taking the two tablets of stone out. Let the truth that God sees be what you believe about yourself as well!

Chapter 25: How God's Word Becomes Inoperative in a Believer's Life

"The farmer sows the word. The ones by the road are the ones where the word is sown; and when they have heard, immediately Satan comes, and takes away the word which has been sown in them. These in the same way are those who are sown on the rocky places, who, when they have heard the word, immediately receive it with joy. They have no root in themselves, but are short-lived. When oppression or persecution arises because of the word, immediately they stumble. Others are those who are sown among the thorns. These are those who have heard the word, and the cares of this age, and the deceitfulness of riches, and the lusts of other things entering in choke the word, and it becomes unfruitful. Those which were sown on the good ground are those who hear the word, and accept it, and bear fruit, some thirty times, some sixty times, and some one hundred times."" (Mark 4:14-20 WEB)

Distraction, intimidation, seduction. These three words summarize the ways Satan tries to make God's word inoperative in people's lives.

He cannot stop the power of God's word after it has matured into a fruit-bearing tree. The only way Satan can hinder God's word is to get you to willingly stop watering that seed.

The first way is distraction. One big source of distraction today is the smartphone. Many fun and interesting apps compete for our attention on a daily basis, distracting us from spending time in God's word.

At church, I see believers using their phones for entertainment while their pastors are preaching on Sundays. This is a form of Satan snatching the word away quickly.

As their hearts are not prioritizing God's word, they miss out on the rhema word of God that can help them in their situation. After the service, they just head to lunch, forgetting most of what the pastor preached.

"Therefore, putting away all filthiness and overflowing of wickedness, receive with humility the implanted word, which is able to save your souls. But be doers of the word, and not only hearers, deluding your own selves. For if anyone is a hearer of the word and not a doer, he is like a man looking at his natural face in a mirror; for he sees himself, and goes away, and immediately forgets what kind of man he was. But he who looks into the perfect law of freedom, and continues, not being a hearer who forgets, but a

doer of the work, this man will be blessed in what he does." (James 1:21-25 WEB)

It is the implanted word of God that has the power to save from every form of trouble. To let the word become effective and powerful in our lives, we must hear with the intention to do it, and not just practice superficial hearing.

If you tend to be distracted by something, remove the source of distraction from you when it is time to receive God's word. This will make it easier for you to focus.

The second way Satan tries to make God's word inoperative in a believer's life is to intimidate him until he stops believing in it.

Have you experienced a situation where you were sick and when you started to read and confess Scriptures about healing, you seemed to get sicker and feel worse than before?

It could be an attempt by the enemy to make you give up on believing God for healing.

A believer who does not know about this Satanic tactic may think, "What's going on? I thought I am supposed to feel better after confessing healing Scriptures, but I feel like my condition is getting worse. Never mind, I'll just stop doing this and rely on the doctor's medicine for healing."

This tactic works on believers who are not rooted in the Gospel—they lack knowledge and understanding about what God's word says. The fear they feel stems from ignorance about their authority over Satan. They also do not understand that God's favor is always upon them because of Jesus' finished work at the cross.

New believers are still prone to trust in their fleshly thoughts and impulses, filling in the gaps of knowledge with their own pre-conceived notions about God.

This is why is important for every believer to consistently receive the preached Gospel. They need to be constantly renewed in their spirit of their mind so that they can mature in their Christian walk.

Finally, there is the tactic of seduction. If Satan cannot distract or intimidate a person, he may try to seduce the person with the lust of the flesh, the lust of the eyes, and the pride of life.

That is how he tempted Eve to eat from the tree of the knowledge of good and evil. He seduced her with the promise that she would become like God, knowing the difference between good and evil.

She saw the fruit that was good for making her wise and touching it did not cause her to die, so she ate.

Satan will observe and see what has the potential to become an idol in a person's heart. Then, Satan will proceed to make the person focus on that thing obsessively so that God is totally forgotten.

For example, if a person loves money, Satan will encourage him to keep chasing money and convince him that there is still a lot of time in the future to devote to God. Money means little to the devil. He will gladly make a person ridiculously rich if that can ruin him.

"But those who are determined to be rich fall into a temptation and a snare and many foolish and harmful lusts, such as drown men in ruin and destruction. For the love of money is a root of all kinds of evil. Some have been led astray from the faith in their greed, and have pierced themselves through with many sorrows. But you, man of God, flee these things, and follow after righteousness, godliness, faith, love, perseverance, and gentleness. Fight the good fight of faith. Take hold of the eternal life to which you were called, and you confessed the good confession in the sight of many witnesses." (1 Timothy 6:9-12 WEB)

A believer will learn either the easy way or the hard way that Jesus is the only one worth focusing on and pursuing.

When you take your eyes off Jesus and pursue something else wholeheartedly, you will be pierced through with many sorrows. Nothing in this world is holistically good enough to satisfy you. Obsessing over the things of this world will just leave you feeling empty. It is vanity of vanities.

Believers who are fruitful are the ones who treasure God's word. They consistently water the good ground of their hearts by receiving the water of God's word.

To "take hold of the eternal life which you were called" is to believe and apply the Gospel truths which you know, recognizing that God's word is the only voice that is one hundred percent true among all the voices in the world.

Receive the seed of God's word by hearing it preached, water it by continuing to receive Gospel truths that reinforce that seed, and you will bear good fruits at the appointed time of harvest.

Are you going to manifest thirty times, sixty times or hundred times of good fruits? If you are not satisfied with thirty times, then keep watering until it matures to sixty times, and then hundred times.

Sow to the Spirit and you will reap life. When you prioritize receiving God's word, the serpent's tactics of distraction, intimidation and seduction will not work against you!

Chapter 26: Let Go and Follow the Holy Spirit

"But I say, walk by the Spirit, and you won't fulfill the lust of the flesh. For the flesh lusts against the Spirit, and the Spirit against the flesh; and these are contrary to one another, that you may not do the things that you desire. But if you are led by the Spirit, you are not under the law." (Galatians 5:16-18 WEB)

Those who trying to discipline their flesh by willpower are playing a tiring game of tug-of-war. They are pulling at one end of the rope while sin in their flesh is pulling at the other end.

The moment you get too burnt out, you fall and get dragged across the floor, straight into a binge session of sin.

Satan wants you playing this game of tug-of-war because he knows you will keep losing.

The flesh is limited in its strength to resist the temptations to sin. It wants to dive right in, but is held back by willpower, like an owner desperately clinging on to a dog who is excitedly barking and chasing someone.

Did you know you that it is just an illusion? You can actually let go of the rope and just walk off. The Holy Spirit is standing right beside you, beckoning you to follow Him.

There is no rope to pull when you are led by the Spirit. He leads you by the hand. You are walking in the same direction, to reach the same goals.

In fact, you will not even feel like you are walking. It will be like being carried by a river, so effortless and yet powerfully effective.

Who are you identifying with—the flesh or the Spirit? When you think that the flesh is you, you will keep lusting against the Spirit. You will have no desire to do what God wants. Serving God will feel like such a chore.

However, when you identify with the Holy Spirit who is joined to your reborn spirit, the opposite will happen: you will lose all desire for the lusts of the flesh.

Sin will disgust you and you will have to be forced to sin—it will be that repulsive to you.

You cannot follow the Spirit when you are still hanging on to that rope.

He wants to lead you somewhere else, so let go of your fleshly attempts to resist sin and follow the Spirit.

Where He is bringing you to, sin cannot follow. The Spirit will lead you so far from sin that you will forget its existence.

In the realm of love, you will be free from fear. It is no longer about resisting sin but following the Holy Spirit and you will automatically abstain from sin!

Chapter 27: Purify your Faith Through Fasting

Many believers are confused about the spiritual activity of fasting. They do not understand its purpose through the lens of the New Covenant of Grace, so they practice it legalistically.

The wrong way to fast is by thinking that God pities you because of how much you are suffering by starving yourself. It is like trying to force Him to help you by harming yourself—a form of emotional blackmail.

No, this is not the purpose of fasting. We know that it is God's will for fasting to continue even under Grace.

"Then John's disciples came to him, saying, "Why do we and the Pharisees fast often, but your disciples don't fast?" Jesus said to them, "Can the friends of the bridegroom mourn, as long as the bridegroom is with them? But the days will come when the bridegroom will be taken away from them, and then they will fast. No one puts a piece of unshrunk cloth on an old

garment; for the patch would tear away from the garment, and a worse hole is made. Neither do people put new wine into old wine skins, or else the skins would burst, and the wine be spilled, and the skins ruined. No, they put new wine into fresh wine skins, and both are preserved."" (Matthew 9:14-17 WEB)

Jesus Himself said that His friends—not just the apostles, but all Christians who are children of God, joint-heirs with Christ—will fast after He is taken away.

The time to fast began after Jesus ascended back to the Father in Heaven. You can be sure that if Jesus has commanded us to fast, it is with the intention of blessing us.

He does not require us to do unnecessary, burdensome things if they will not benefit in any way. His heart is for us to live the abundant life through having faith in Him.

"For my yoke is easy, and my burden is light."" (Matthew 11:30 WEB)

Why did Jesus give the example of the garment and the wine skins? He was responding to John's disciples' question. He meant that yes, Christians will fast, but not for the purpose of mourning about God's judgment against Israel and showing outward repentance for their sins like the Pharisees.

This new approach to fasting would not be the same as Old Covenant fasting. It would be a New Covenant fasting that is for the benefit of the Christian who practices it as led by the Holy Spirit.

In Jesus' analogy, the patch tearing away from the garment causing a bigger hole and the wine skins bursting is telling us that we cannot mix the Old and New covenants together. It would end up becoming unprofitable for us.

Fasting would be to no effect for us if we do it with an Old Covenant mentality—it would just be voluntary starvation, without any benefits.

I mean, you might shed some pounds and detox your body, but those are just the natural benefits, not the spiritual ones.

We also see the disciples in the early church fasting when they wanted guidance from the Holy Spirit, so it is clearly a New Covenant practice.

"Now in the assembly that was at Antioch there were some prophets and teachers: Barnabas, Simeon who was called Niger, Lucius of Cyrene, Manaen the foster brother of Herod the tetrarch, and Saul. As they served the Lord and fasted, the Holy Spirit said, "Separate Barnabas and Saul for me, for the work to which I have called them." Then, when they had fasted and prayed and laid their hands on them, they sent them away." (Acts 13:1-3 WEB)

What fasting also does is that it casts the unbelief out of your heart so that you can receive the promises of God easily without hindrances from the flesh. This is why prayer when combined with fasting is extremely powerful and lethal against the enemy's strongholds.

"One of the multitude answered, "Teacher, I brought to you my son, who has a mute spirit; and wherever it seizes him, it throws him down, and he foams at the mouth, and grinds his teeth, and wastes away. I asked your disciples to cast it out, and they weren't able." He answered him, "Unbelieving generation, how long shall I be with you? How long shall I bear with you? Bring him to me." They brought him to him, and when he saw him, immediately the spirit convulsed him, and he fell on the ground, wallowing and foaming at the mouth. He asked his father, "How long has it been since this has come to him?" He said, "From childhood. Often it has cast him both into the fire and into the water, to destroy him. But if you can do anything, have compassion on us, and help us." Jesus said to him, "If you can believe, all things are possible to him who believes." Immediately the father of the child cried out with tears, "I believe. Help my unbelief!" When Jesus saw that a multitude came running together, he rebuked the unclean spirit, saying to him, "You mute and deaf spirit, I command you, come out of him, and never enter him again!" Having cried out, and convulsed greatly, it came out of him. The boy became like one dead; so much that most of them said, "He is dead." But Jesus took him by the hand, and raised him up; and he arose. When he had come into the house, his disciples asked him privately, "Why couldn't we cast it out?" He said to them, "This kind can come out by nothing, except by prayer and fasting.""" (Mark 9:17-29 WEB)

As we can see from the passage on the previous page, Jesus' disciples could not cast the demon out of the boy because they had unbelief.

Jesus did not mean that prayer and fasting have a combined special power to cast stronger types of demons out, but rather, the spiritual activities of prayer and fasting help us to rid our hearts of unbelief.

We cannot receive from God if we pray with unbelief. You do not need huge faith— you just need faith the size of a mustard seed (that is really little) and the absence of unbelief.

When we fast, we grow closer to God and less dependent on our own flesh. We learn to trust Him promptly and live by faith instead of by sight.

The apostles could not cast the demon out because it was convulsing the boy, causing them to revert to sight instead of staying strong in faith.

But when you fast as led by the Holy Spirit, you become more anchored to the realm of faith than the realm of sight.

Do you remember how it feels like to eat a huge meal and feel so sluggish and lethargic afterwards? It is like all the resources in your flesh are channelled to do the work of digestion. The flesh becomes the king in this case.

However, such hindrances are gone when you are fasting. The flesh is brought into submission and it is a time for the spirit to be in charge.

It is just you and God without the loud noise of the flesh. Can you see how it is easier to reach the state of pure faith through fasting?

Sometimes, the Holy Spirit will lead you to fast. You will suddenly have the desire to do it. Be promptly obedient to that Spirit-led desire.

He could use that fast to break Satanic bondages in your life when you reach the unhindered state of faith. You will also hear Him clearer than before.

As you can see, fasting is also a spiritual weapon we have to silence the serpent!

Chapter 28: Look Beyond the Stone

"Now on the next day, which was the day after the Preparation Day, the chief priests and the Pharisees were gathered together to Pilate, saying, "Sir, we remember what that deceiver said while he was still alive: 'After three days I will rise again.' Command therefore that the tomb be made secure until the third day, lest perhaps his disciples come at night and steal him away, and tell the people, 'He is risen from the dead;' and the last deception will be worse than the first." Pilate said to them, "You have a guard. Go, make it as secure as you can." So they went with the guard and made the tomb secure, sealing the stone." (Matthew 27:62-66 WEB)

I believe that the chief priests and Pharisees believed deep down that Jesus could possibly rise again from the dead.

They knew the Old Testament Scriptures well and could see that Jesus did the miracles that the Messiah was prophesied to do. For example, no one had healed a Jewish leper in Israel before until Jesus came. No one until then had opened the eyes of the blind. These were clear Messianic miracles.

To serve their evil purpose of keeping their religious power even though it was just an empty shell, the chiefs priests and Pharisees could not tell Pontius Pilate that Jesus is probably the Messiah and that He has the power to rise from the dead.

They have to concoct a believable excuse to get Pilate's help to make the tomb more secure.

Out of fear, they probably plotted to seal Jesus inside the tomb if He resurrected, by blocking the entrance with a huge stone and stationing guards there to stop Him from escaping.

The stone is so heavy that it is impossible for one man to move it aside. The stone is also a picture of the Ten Commandments written on the two tablets of stone.

Satan is so afraid that you realize that you are a resurrected being. He has stationed demons and prepared deceptions to keep you trapped in the dark tomb of fear and ignorance.

As long as you are focused on the huge heavy stone (the Ten Commandments), it will be an obstacle to you, and you cannot leave the tomb even though you are a resurrected being. You have to look through and beyond the stone.

"Behold, there was a great earthquake, for an angel of the Lord descended from the sky, and came and rolled away the stone from the door, and sat on it...As they went to tell his disciples, behold, Jesus met them, saying,

"Rejoice!" They came and took hold of his feet, and worshiped him."
(Matthew 28:2, 9 WEB)

The angel rolled away the stone not for Jesus to leave the tomb, as we can see from the passage that He was already outside, ready to meet the women. The angel removed the stone for the disciples to go in and see that Jesus is indeed risen.

The stone did not bother Jesus—He just passed through it. His resurrected body transcends the natural laws of the world. It can pass through solid objects, travel faster than the speed of light, and yet still do things like eat. It also has flesh and bones.

Likewise, when Satan tries to trap you with the Ten Commandments, just see through that deception and walk right through it. To go back under the Law is to regress. We have come under the New Covenant of Grace which exceeds the Old Covenant of the Law.

Walk through the stone, and into the glorious light which is to live in the revelation of Grace.

When you are Law conscious, it is like being stuck in a small dark tomb. My wife and I visited the "Garden Tomb" in Jerusalem and the alleged site of the tomb that Jesus was buried in. The tomb is like the size of half a bedroom. Imagine living permanently in a confined place like that.

People under the Law live very small lives because of fear and self-imposed restrictions. They are so afraid of getting punished by God and attacked by the enemy that they are in the mode of avoiding things needlessly.

But when you step out of the dark tomb, it is a vast world outside illuminated by sunlight. That is what the New Covenant of Grace is. It gives true freedom, and it leads to a broad life with God.

"But if the ministry of death, written and engraved on stones, was glorious, so that the children of Israel could not look steadily at the face of Moses because of the glory of his countenance, which glory was passing away, how will the ministry of the Spirit not be more glorious?" (II Corinthians 3:7-8 NKJV)

To look beyond the stone means to see that Jesus' finished work at the cross has freed you from the Law which Paul calls the "ministry of death".

You can see beyond what has already passed, and clearly understand that you are now under the "ministry of the Spirit".

Follow the Holy Spirit, and He will show you a miraculous life, and how to have dominion over the serpent because you are under Grace!

Chapter 29: Be Careful How You Hear

"They took hold of him, and brought him to the Areopagus, saying, "May we know what this new teaching is, which is spoken by you? For you bring certain strange things to our ears. We want to know therefore what these things mean." Now all the Athenians and the strangers living there spent their time in nothing else, but either to tell or to hear some new thing." (Acts 17:19-21 WEB)

In the Bible, we see different attitudes of people who hear God's word. When introduced to the Gospel, the Athenians wanted to know about it for the sake of hearing something new and interesting. It was a form of entertainment for them, to relieve their boredom.

"For the time will come when they will not listen to the sound doctrine, but, having itching ears, will heap up for themselves teachers after their own lusts;

and will turn away their ears from the truth, and turn aside to fables." (2 Timothy 4:3-4 WEB)

Paul calls this type of hearer as having "itching ears"—the urge to hear something new just to relieve the uncomfortable boredom of daily routine.

The Gospel of Jesus Christ is not just a story for entertainment. It is the only truth that saves and delivers.

"The brothers immediately sent Paul and Silas away by night to Beroea. When they arrived, they went into the Jewish synagogue. Now these were more noble than those in Thessalonica, in that they received the word with all readiness of mind, examining the Scriptures daily to see whether these things were so. Many of them therefore believed; also of the prominent Greek women, and not a few men." (Acts 17:10-12 WEB)

The unbelieving Jews in Thessalonica openly and deliberately persecuted those who preached the Gospel, but if you are a believer, you definitely will not do that.

The Jews in Beroea were more open-minded towards Paul's preaching. Most importantly, they examined the Scriptures themselves to see if Paul's teachings aligned with the Scriptures. Many of them believed the Gospel and were saved. The Holy Spirit calls these Beroeans "noble".

It is not just about hearing a new revelation—you have to check if it contradicts God's word. Many believers are fooled by erroneous and even demonic teachings that seduce the flesh because they do not bother to examine their Bibles to see if what their pastors teach them is true or not.

Having this sort of spiritual slothfulness is like eating a bowl of food without looking at what you are scooping up in your spoon. What if there is fecal matter, an insect, or a huge fish bone? We need to inspect what we are feeding on.

Even if the food is good, you need to chew your food too. We chew our spiritual food by meditating on the teachings that we receive. This way, we digest it better and benefit more from the word. It is not just hearing and forgetting, but we hear and then go all the way to apply it, becoming noble doers of the Word.

Satan wants to quickly snatch away the word from your heart. Influencing your attitude towards hearing God's word can be one tactic he uses. Do you find yourself only looking out for something new and interesting when hearing sermons? Do you tune out when you think you have heard it all before?

Grains (carbohydrates) are part of man's staple diet. You cannot just say that you already ate that yesterday. You need it again today. Likewise, the foundational Gospel truths that you heard before need to be received repeatedly—we need the nourishment and have the tendency to forget to apply it.

There is this saying, "Out of sight, out of mind". When you are not hearing a truth, you will end up forgetting it, no matter how basic it seems. We need to keep hearing the Gospel (every aspect of it) so that Jesus is always at the forefront of our hearts and minds.

"Be careful therefore how you hear. For whoever has, to him will be given; and whoever doesn't have, from him will be taken away even that which he thinks he has."" (Luke 8:18 WEB)

As Jesus said, we must be carefully how we hear. Our attitude towards receiving God's word should be like a hungry person about to have dinner: open your mouth (an open mind), look at your spoon (compare the preached word to the written Scriptures), and chew your food (meditate on the truths that you hear).

The digested food then becomes energy (God's power—the result of the word mixed with faith) which is released by working (speaking words and doing actions of faith).

If you have a keen heart to hear God's word, you will receive revelations of Jesus, and more will be given to you as you keep hearing and hearing. Praise Jesus for a hearing heart that is the good ground for seeds of God's word to be sown in!

Chapter 30: What Satan Says About you Does Not Matter

"Even though I walk through the valley of the shadow of death, I will fear no evil, for you are with me. Your rod and your staff, they comfort me." (Psalms 23:4 WEB)

In previous chapters, we have examined the many spiritual weapons that God has equipped us with, and also the abundant angelic protection we have from Him.

In Psalm 23, David wrote about the valley of the shadow of death, which represents any dark, gloomy season in our journey of life.

Even in such seasons, there is no need to fear because Jesus your Good Shepherd is still with you. So not only are you equipped with spiritual weapons and protected by angels, but God Himself is always with you.

"I am the good shepherd. The good shepherd lays down his life for the sheep."
(John 10:11 WEB)

I am so glad that Jesus is the God who holds a rod and a staff. The rod is for guiding us who are His flock of sheep, and the staff doubles up as a weapon to defend us from the enemy.

A shepherd's rod usually has a curved end for hooking the sheep who are wandering off. When we wander away from the right path into dangerous situations, Jesus lovingly directs us back through the Holy Spirit.

When Satan comes close as a wolf or roaring lion to attack, he gets whacked away with the shepherd's staff. The enemy attacks but is never allowed to go beyond boundaries that God has set.

"marked out for it my bound, set bars and doors, and said, 'Here you may come, but no further. Here your proud waves shall be stayed?'" (Job 38:10-11 WEB)

The Lord spoke the words above to Job. He was talking about how He set boundaries for the waves of the sea. God is a God of order. He does everything in an orderly fashion, setting them in times and seasons, and determining precise boundaries for them.

Similarly, to Satan, God says, "This is as close as you can come, no further. Here, your proud attacks will be stopped."

We hear of Christians that died in tragic ways. However, these are not successes of the enemy, but choices made by the Christians themselves. Satan has no power to kill a believer, but he may deceive one to choose that path himself.

"Women received their dead by resurrection. Others were tortured, not accepting their deliverance, that they might obtain a better resurrection." (Hebrews 11:35 WEB)

No matter how dire your situation is, if you pray to God and believe for deliverance, you will surely be saved. Nothing is impossible for our God who raises the dead.

But He also gives you the choice to reject deliverance and go to Heaven—to finally be free from this earthly sojourn and to rest in the heavenly Paradise.

The "better resurrection" that the verse above talks about is the Rapture of the saints (in Greek: "harpazo" which means to snatch away), whereby believers who have fallen asleep in death will be resurrected first before receiving their new glorified bodies.

It is so comforting to know that Satan is just a liar who can only destroy within boundaries. He cannot just decide to kill you one day and do it.

It is even more assuring to know that Jesus personally protects us, and this is the sole reason that we do not have to be afraid of evil.

The serpent is weaker than you think he is, and you have more authority over him and your own life than you think. What Satan says about you does not matter.

He can try to shoot fiery darts of condemnation and accusations, but they will be extinguished if you do not believe them. It is what you say about yourself that has an effect.

After silencing the serpent, what are you going to say about yourself and your life? It is ultimately what you choose to say and believe that determines how much you reign in this lifetime!

Chapter 31: Be Strong in the Lord, Not in the Flesh

"Finally, be strong in the Lord, and in the strength of his might. Put on the whole armor of God, that you may be able to stand against the wiles of the devil. For our wrestling is not against flesh and blood, but against the principalities, against the powers, against the world's rulers of the darkness of this age, and against the spiritual forces of wickedness in the heavenly places. Therefore put on the whole armor of God, that you may be able to withstand in the evil day, and, having done all, to stand." (Ephesians 6:10-13 WEB)

I cannot imagine a book about spiritual warfare without delving into the whole armor of God. Now I feel that the Holy Spirit wants to shine light on this area.

Our tendency is to be strong in the flesh and in our own might.

The most visible representation of this is a person who regularly goes to the gym to work out, combining that with a disciplined diet to complement muscle growth.

If someone does that to protect himself from any possible attackers, or to look physically good so that he can earn favor or approval from people, his trust is in fleshly might.

I am not saying it is wrong to exercise or eat a healthy diet—I do those too. They are beneficial for your body, but when you start believing that strength is found in the flesh instead of in the Lord, you are setting yourself up for unnecessary falls and painful lessons.

It is much easier to trust in the flesh when your flesh is strong, so that is the danger. A physically weak person who thinks that he is powerless will find it much easier to rely on the Lord because he knows he has no strength of his own.

As the passage on the previous page says, your true enemies are not fellow humans, but rather Satan and his hierarchy of demons. You cannot defeat a spirit with fleshly weapons.

No matter how strong your willpower is, how disciplined you are, how logically smart or physically strong, you will lose in spiritual warfare by relying on the flesh.

Our enemy is a wily devil. He is that cunning serpent who caused Adam and Eve to sin in the Garden of Eden. Deception, distraction, and intimidation are his main weapons of choice today.

If we want to stand and not fall, we need to put on the whole armor of God. As mentioned in an earlier chapter, "whole armor" in Greek is panoplía (from pás, "every" and hóplon, "weapon"), meaning a complete set of defensive and offensive armor (weapons), i.e. everything needed to wage successful warfare.

It refers to the full resources the Lord gives to believers so they can successfully wage spiritual warfare. In this way they do not fight for victory—but from His victory!

We put on these pieces of armor not by using our hands and feet, but through faith—believing in our heart and speaking with our mouths.

I believe the Holy Spirit inspired Paul to teach about the whole armor of God based on this Old Testament verse:

"He put on righteousness as a breastplate, and a helmet of salvation on his head. He put on garments of vengeance for clothing, and was clad with zeal as a mantle." (Isaiah 59:17 WEB)

You may notice that Paul also talks about the breastplate of righteousness and the helmet of salvation.

Instead of the garments of vengeance which is not ours to wear (vengeance belongs to the Lord), Paul's version elaborates on the seven pieces that we need.

In the following chapters, we will study the individual pieces of the whole armor of God, so that you will be fully prepared for spiritual warfare!

Chapter 32: Gird Up your Loins with the Truth

"Stand, therefore, having your loins girt about in truth..." (Ephesians 6:14a YLT98)

Back in Paul's time, men wore long flowing tunics, making it hard to do heavy manual work or to battle while wearing it.

So, the men would gather up the hems of the garments and tie it up into a knot in front of the waist to essentially transform it into something like shorts.

Asking someone to gird up your loins is as good as saying, "Prepare for battle," or "Prepare for hard work".

What is truth? Truth is Jesus, which is also termed the Gospel of Jesus Christ—everything good from God that mankind can enjoy because of Jesus' finished work at the cross.

"Jesus said to him, "I am the way, the truth, and the life. No one comes to the Father, except through me." (John 14:6 WEB)

Without being established in truth, it is like trying to wage spiritual warfare with the hem of your tunic being a hindrance—you cannot move about freely, and you may clumsily trip over your own clothes.

In other words, being ignorant about what the Scriptures teach about the Gospel is self-sabotage and making it hard to battle against the serpent.

Think about how swiftly a serpent can glide around on the ground. It is very elusive, and you cannot kill it easily when you are tripping over your own robes.

When Satan shoots a flaming arrow of deception and condemnation at you, it will be hard to dodge when you are not girded with the truth.

How do you gird yourself with the truth? By growing in your understanding and knowledge of God's word. Whenever you read the Word, hear a sermon, these are activities that function like girding your loins with the truth.

As you run and bend, the knot will get loose and eventually the hem of your garment will fall back down to your shins again. It is not enough to hear the Gospel once because as you go about your day-to-day life, you will end up forgetting—other thoughts from the world and your own flesh will replace the truth if you do not keep it fresh in your mind.

Stay tightly girded by making it a priority to hear the Gospel of Jesus Christ. When you are consistent in that, you will always be in a battle-ready state!

Chapter 33: Guard your Heart with the Breastplate of Righteousness

"...and having put on the breastplate of righteousness," (Ephesians 6:14b WEB)

What is the most precious part of your body that is protected by a breastplate? It would be the heart of course.

Righteousness does not come by works, but it is a gift that we received. Jesus is our righteousness—positionally, we are as righteous as He is because we are in Christ.

When you see yourself clothed with righteousness as a gift, your heart is protected from worries and fears.

As we previously examined, one of Satan's tactics is to bind believers with the bronze fetters of worry, fear, and self-condemnation.

You will only fall prey to these traps when you are not actively wearing the breastplate of righteousness—when you are living by works-based righteousness and not the gift of righteousness.

When you think God favors you when you are obedient and that His wrath and curse are upon you when you sin, then your heart is left totally exposed to Satan.

"Keep your heart with all diligence, for out of it is the wellspring of life." (Proverbs 4:23 WEB)

Satan wants to attack your heart because what you believe determines what you speak, and therefore what fruits you reap in your life. The heart is the source of realities you see in your life.

In the state of depending on your works, it is easy to crush you emotionally. All it takes is some accusations and you will torture yourself with self-condemnation, speaking words of death upon yourself to reap the fruit of death in your life.

On the other hand, if you actively wear the breastplate of righteousness by relying on the gift of righteousness, Satan's lies and accusations cannot affect you.

Satan may come saying, "You just sinned. How can you expect God to bless your business? How can you think that He will keep you and your family healthy and safe? No, He is angry with you until you confess all your sins and make things right by doing enough good works to balance out the scales."

You can boldly confess, "God blesses me not based on my obedience, but based on Jesus' perfect obedience at the cross. Provision, health, healing, protection are all blessings purchased by the precious blood of Jesus. It has nothing to do with my works. I am still blessed and righteous in Christ!"

Do you see how the breastplate of righteousness is so important? Never go a day without it!

Chapter 34: Go Further Safely with the Gospel of Peace

"and having fitted your feet with the preparation of the Good News of peace;" (Ephesians 6:15 WEB)

In Paul's illustration, he compares the Good News (Gospel) of peace with a pair of sandals.

Imagine running around and battling without wearing any footwear. The ground has sharp rocks and all sorts of dangerous things you may injure your feet on. However, when you wear sandals, you will not dash your foot again a stone.

"For he will put his angels in charge of you, to guard you in all your ways. They will bear you up in their hands, so that you won't dash your foot

against a stone. You will tread on the lion and cobra. You will trample the young lion and the serpent underfoot." (Psalms 91:11-13 WEB)

Believing in the Gospel of peace is what activates angels to guard you in all your ways. It also empowers you to tread upon demons (represented by the lion and serpent)—Satan who is the roaring lion and the ancient serpent will have no advantage in your life.

The Gospel is also called the Gospel of Grace and the Gospel of Christ, so why does Paul choose the word "peace" in this case? It is this aspect of peace that protects us in our daily walk. The peace refers to having peace with God. That is the good news.

"and through him to reconcile all things to himself, by him, whether things on the earth, or things in the heavens, having made peace through the blood of his cross." (Colossians 1:20 WEB)

You actively wear the Gospel of peace as sandals by believing that you have peace with God because of the blood of Jesus. When you are conscious that God is at peace with you, you can freely receive His protection and favor.

By wearing fitting sandals, you will be able to run further and faster than going barefoot. Believing that you are at peace with God because of Jesus' finished work at the cross allows you to freely receive the grace and favor to do more than others who feel that they can only rely on themselves.

"But by the grace of God I am what I am. His grace which was given to me was not futile, but I worked more than all of them; yet not I, but the grace of God which was with me." (1 Corinthians 15:10 WEB)

The apostle Paul had a great revelation of the Gospel of Peace, so he was able to freely receive and use the grace of God which was with him. Just read the Book of Acts and you will see the amazing exploits Paul did through God's Grace.

"Grace to you and peace be multiplied in the knowledge of God and of Jesus our Lord," (2 Peter 1:2 WEB)

The more you know (as a revelation in your heart) that you have peace with God, the more grace and shalom peace are multiplied in your life.

Are you running around barefoot every day, making yourself vulnerable to harm, or will you put on the Gospel of peace and run faster and further than you ever could before? Always wear your trusty sandals!

Chapter 35: How to Use the Shield of the Faith

"above all, having taken up the shield of the faith, in which ye shall be able all the fiery darts of the evil one to quench," (Ephesians 6:16 YLT98)

Many English translations of the verse above omit the word "the" before the word "faith". If you look at the original Greek, there is a "tēs" which means "the (referring to the definite article)".

If you do a simple search of "the faith" in the New Testament, it almost always refers to the faith in Christ Jesus, which is the Gospel of Jesus Christ in its totality.

"But after some days, Felix came with Drusilla, his wife, who was a Jewess, and sent for Paul, and heard him concerning the faith in Christ Jesus." (Acts 24:24 WEB)

In Ephesians 6:16 as seen on the previous page, "having taken up" is in the aorist tense which means an action that has already been completed in the past.

Paul was addressing all the believers in the Ephesian church. This means that "the shield of the faith" is taken up the moment a person becomes a born-again believer by placing his or her faith in Jesus as Lord.

If you are a believer, the first step is to know that you are already holding the shield of the faith. Next, is to learn how to use that shield to actually quench Satan's fiery darts.

These fiery darts are not literal. Satan attacks spiritually first to produce harm both spiritually and physically. These fiery darts are the condemning accusations and lies that he shoots at you.

When he whispers in your ear that God hates you because you keep sinning despite Him giving His Grace every day, that is a fiery dart. If you accept that thought by believing and speaking it, then you got injured by the fiery dart.

I wrote a Christian fiction novel featuring pieces of the armor of God as spiritual weapons that have shape and form.

For the shield of the faith, I depicted it as a watery shield because it is supposed to quench Satan's fiery darts, which is what water does to fire. If it is a metal shield, fire would make the shield too hot to hold!

Picture this: when Satan shoots a fiery dart your way, to use the shield of the faith, the dart would have to hit the shield. This represents Satan sending a thought into your mind, but it is unable to enter your heart because your faith in the Gospel rejects the Satanic thought. The fiery dart is quenched, and just drops to the ground.

Therefore, to use the shield of the faith, you simply retrieve a Gospel truth that you believe in your heart which disproves Satan's lies, and then you confess that truth with your mouth.

For example, when Satan uses a person in your life as a mouthpiece to say, "You will never amount to anything in life. You are always going to be a useless bum," you can reject that thought and confess, "No, Jeremiah 29:11 tells me that because I am in Christ, I can confidently hope that God has prepared a good future for me. Proverbs 4:18 tells me that because I am righteous in Christ, my path will shine brighter and brighter!"

In the case of quenching Satan's fiery darts, the Gospel of Jesus Christ acts as a defensive shield.

In other instances, when you are the one initiating an attack upon Satanic strongholds, it acts as an offensive sword, as we have examined earlier on in this book.

What a versatile weapon we have, and it is so simple for us to use!

Chapter 36: Wear Hope like a Helmet

"and the helmet of the salvation receive..." (Ephesians 6:17a YLT98)

Like "the shield of the faith", many translations omit "the" in front of the word "salvation" in the verse above. "The salvation" refers to being saved by Grace through faith in Jesus Christ.

"for by grace you have been saved through faith, and that not of yourselves; it is the gift of God, not of works, that no one would boast." (Ephesians 2:8-9 WEB)

To receive the helmet of the salvation is to fill your mind with the hope of the receiving the salvation we have in Christ—not just salvation from Hell, but its full array of its benefits.

The word translated as "salvation" comes from the Greek word "sōtēria" which has all-encompassing meanings of "welfare, prosperity, deliverance, preservation, salvation and safety."

"But let us, since we belong to the day, be sober, putting on the breastplate of faith and love, and, for a helmet, the hope of salvation. For God didn't appoint us to wrath, but to the obtaining of salvation through our Lord Jesus Christ, who died for us, that, whether we wake or sleep, we should live together with him. Therefore exhort one another, and build each other up, even as you also do." (1 Thessalonians 5:8-11 WEB)

When you receive the helmet of the salvation, it means that you are actively expecting good things to happen in your life because you are saved in Christ.

For us who are saved, "hope" is not just wishful thinking or based on computations of natural probabilities. HELPS Word-studies defines hope (in Greek: elpis) as an expectation of what is sure.

According to the passage above, when you wear the hope of salvation as a helmet, you will know that God has not appointed you to wrath and that you will surely obtain salvation in the fullest sense of the word.

Depression is a mental condition where you have an expectation of bad things to come, while having hope in Christ is the opposite. It is having a confident expectation of good things to come. When your helmet is on, your mind will be protected from Satan's negative and evil thoughts.

There is a hope of all hopes we are told to look forward to which is the hope of Jesus' return and our bodily redemption. That is what the passage on the previous page is talking about.

Whether we are alive or asleep (because of physical death) when Jesus returns for us, we will still receive new glorified bodies and live with Jesus forever.

"looking for the blessed hope and appearing of the glory of our great God and Savior, Jesus Christ;" (Titus 2:13 WEB)

Garrison your mind with hope like how a helmet protects your head. You are in Christ, so you can always confidently expect good things to come!

Chapter 37: Prayer—The Final Piece of the Whole Armor of God

"and the helmet of the salvation receive, and the sword of the Spirit, which is the saying of God, through all prayer and supplication praying at all times in the Spirit, and in regard to this same, watching in all perseverance and supplication for all the saints —" (Ephesians 6:17-18 YLT98)

If you read the passage above in the original Greek, you will see that there is a "dia" before "all prayer and supplication". Dia means "through" and many Bible translations omit this word.

However, the "through" is important because it teaches us how to receive the helmet of salvation and the sword of the Spirit. We receive them through prayer.

The sword of the Spirit is the "saying of God" (In Greek: rhēma Theou) which means what God is currently saying to you.

It is interesting that the passage above suggests that God will speak to you when you pray. If you want to hear God saying something to you, pray—speak to Him, and He will speak to you. It is a two-way dialogue between living persons. A Father and His child having a real conversation.

Prayer is a generic term for communication with God. But supplication is when you make specific requests for His help. Then, praying in the Spirit is the same thing as praying in tongues which is a spiritual gift of the Holy Spirit.

Praying is the way to protect your mind from the enemy's negative thoughts and it is also the way to deliver an offensive blow to Satanic strongholds.

The apostle Paul instructed believers to offer prayers and supplication, but what he asked them to do "at all times" is to pray in the Spirit.

It is so relaxing and easy to pray in tongues, and when you pray in tongues at all times, it is like God and you working in sync. He works through your spoken agreement. Even though you do not understand what you are saying, you are praying His perfect will to pass.

When you pray in tongues at all times, you are simultaneously attacking and defending. The Holy Spirit gives you the utterances to destroy what is of Satan, and to protect yourself and even others from Satanic traps and oppressions.

Personally, I notice that after I pray in tongues, good ideas come to me. God speaks and gives me His wisdom. I receive the "saying of God" which is the sword of the Spirit, empowering me to cut through the works of the enemy.

I believe that Satan hates the gift of praying in tongues. He does not understand what you are saying, and he has no defence against the power of perfect prayers offered up in perfect faith.

He cannot withstand a believer who is praying in tongues, so the only thing Satan can do is to discourage you from continuing to pray in tongues.

Even nowadays, the thought that "Maybe you're just making it up...are you sure that you're even praying, or you're just speaking nonsense," still enters my mind once in a while. These are obviously external thoughts whispered to me by demons because they use the second-person pronoun "you". They do this to try and discourage me from praying in tongues.

However, I cannot doubt the gift of praying in tongues because there have been too many miraculous happenings that have occurred when I use this spiritual gift. There is no doubt that it is real, and it is powerful.

When Satan tries hard to stop you from doing something—when you sense a lot of demonic opposition, there must be a lot of good that can come out of doing that.

It is fun to play the 'opposite game' with Satan. Whatever he wants you to stop doing, you should double up on doing it because he is indirectly pointing you to something powerful.

No one sends robbers to rob an empty house. If you see robbers, it is because there is something valuable that they want to steal.

There you have it—we have covered all seven pieces of the whole armor of God: the girdle of truth, the breastplate of righteousness, the sandals of the Gospel of peace, the shield of the faith, the helmet of the salvation, the sword of the Spirit, and finally, prayer (including praying in the Spirit).

The first five are defensive, while the last two are offensive. When you understand how to put on and use the whole armor of God, you will be well-equipped to silence the serpent and emerge victorious in spiritual warfare!

Chapter 38: You are Blessed—Satan Cannot Curse You

"He sent messengers to Balaam the son of Beor, to Pethor, which is by the River, to the land of the children of his people, to call him, saying, "Behold, there is a people who came out of Egypt. Behold, they cover the surface of the earth, and they are staying opposite me. Please come now therefore curse me this people; for they are too mighty for me. Perhaps I shall prevail, that we may strike them, and that I may drive them out of the land; for I know that he whom you bless is blessed, and he whom you curse is cursed."" (Numbers 22:5-6 WEB)

There was once a prophet-for-hire called Balaam. He was renowned for his ability to cast effective enchantments upon people. There was an anointing upon Balaam, but he abused it for monetary gain.

Balak, the King of Moab, hired Balaam to curse Israel, to weaken them so that he might destroy them.

Balaam's case is very interesting because he was in direct contact with God, even though he was abusing the calling and anointing upon his life.

But Balaam was not free to do whatever he wanted. It seems that the power is only released for what God allows him to do.

"God said to Balaam, "You shall not go with them. You shall not curse the people; for they are blessed.""" (Numbers 22:12 WEB)

Whoever God calls blessed cannot be cursed. Even if the most notorious enchanter tries to cast an evil spell upon you, it will not work because God will negate that curse.

"Blessed be the God and Father of our Lord Jesus Christ, who has blessed us with every spiritual blessing in the heavenly places in Christ;" (Ephesians 1:3 WEB)

In Christ, we have been blessed with every spiritual blessing. We who were formerly Gentiles have been engrafted into the eternal nation of Israel.

"Behold, I have received a command to bless. He has blessed, and I can't reverse it. He has not seen iniquity in Jacob. Neither has he seen perverseness in Israel. Yahweh his God is with him. The shout of a king is

among them. God brings them out of Egypt. He has as it were the strength of the wild ox. Surely there is no enchantment with Jacob; Neither is there any divination with Israel. Now it shall be said of Jacob and of Israel, 'What has God done!'" (Numbers 23:20-23 WEB)

God has commanded the blessing upon you, so no magician nor demon can reverse that by cursing you.

When God looks at you, He does not see iniquity or perverseness, because He sees you perfectly clean in Christ—you are washed with His blood, free from the taint of sin.

When someone threatens to cast black magic or voodoo spells on you, do not fear. These demonic weapons will not work on you.

In fact, pray for mercy upon the spell-caster because the spell may rebound and hit him much harder!

"Whoever digs a pit shall fall into it. Whoever rolls a stone, it will come back on him." (Proverbs 26:27 WEB)

The first murderer who was a man is Cain. After Cain killed his brother Abel, God placed a protective mark upon Cain.

This mark ensured that whoever killed Cain would receive a seven times worse punishment from God.

"Cain said to the LORD, "My punishment is greater than I can bear. Behold, You have driven me out this day from the face of the land; and from

Your face (presence) I will be hidden, and I will be a fugitive and an [aimless] vagabond on the earth, and whoever finds me will kill me." And the LORD said to him, "Therefore, whoever kills Cain, a sevenfold vengeance [that is, punishment seven times worse] shall be taken on him [by Me]." And the LORD set a [protective] mark (sign) on Cain, so that no one who found (met) him would kill him." (Genesis 4:13-15 AMP)

Everyone who saw this supernatural mark stayed clear from Cain because they did not want any trouble for themselves.

Did you know that there is a spiritual mark on you too? God's seal is on your forehead, and that is how demons know whether you are a believer or not.

If God gave a murderer like Cain a sevenfold assurance of protection, then the protection upon you, precious child of God, is much more.

"They were told that they should not hurt the grass of the earth, neither any green thing, neither any tree, but only those people who don't have God's seal on their foreheads." (Revelation 9:4 WEB)

When demons see God's seal on you, they will not dare to try and curse you, because the rebounding punishment will be more than seven times worse!

Parting Words

Thanks for reading this book—all glory goes to our Lord Jesus Christ!

Through this book "Silencing the Serpent", we have examined the different ways that Satan deceives, tempts, seduced, intimidates and blinds people.

You cannot be cursed directly. Satan knows he cannot attack you blatantly, but he works subtly, feeding you with deceptive thoughts that grow into Satanic strongholds when you believe and accept them.

The only one who can curse you is yourself. If you sow words of death into your own life and if you put yourself under the works of the Law, it is subjecting yourself to curses.

Dear child of God, if you diligently read this book and receive the truths within as revelations in your heart, you will be ready for spiritual warfare. Put on the whole armor of God every day.

Equip yourself with the powerful spiritual weapons in your arsenal. Every time you wake up, let demons tremble, and say, "Oh no, that person is awake again!"

I believe that as you apply the truths shared in this book, you will silence the serpent in your life!

If you were blessed by this book, kindly send me a testimony by email to miltongoh1993@gmail.com

You can also read my blog for more new and exciting Christian content at http://miltongoh.net

If the Holy Spirit leads you to do so, you can partner financially with my ministry by joining us as a patron. This is the link: http://patreon.com/miltongohblog

As a patron, you will receive exclusive rewards like my eBooks, sermon notes, original devotionals, be added to a WhatsApp Bible Study Group where I share daily takeaways from the Bible and be part of an amazing community of Bible-believing, revelation-seeking Christians.

Not a believer yet? If you have decided to receive Jesus Christ as the Lord and Savior of your life, speak the following prayer and believe in your heart—it will definitely work for you.

You may or may not feel any observable change immediately after praying this, but you will be saved! Congratulations on making the best decision of your life!

"Father in heaven, I come to you in the name of Jesus. I confess that I am a sinner, and I repent of my sins and the life that I have lived. I receive your complete forgiveness.

I believe that your only begotten Son Jesus Christ shed His precious blood on the cross at Calvary and died for my sins and I am now willing to turn from my sin.

You said in the Scriptures that if we confess the Lord our God and believe in our hearts that God raised Jesus from the dead, we shall be saved.

I believe that God raised Jesus from the dead. Right now, I confess Jesus as the Lord of my life. I accept Jesus Christ as my own personal Savior and according to His Word, right now I am saved.

Lord Jesus, transform my life so that I may bring glory and honor to you alone and not to myself.

Thank you, Jesus, for dying for me and giving me eternal life. Amen."

Made in the USA
Columbia, SC
27 August 2024